A TALE OF
TWO BURGHS
the archaeology of Old and New Aberdeen

ABERDEEN ART GALLERY & MUSEUMS

A TALE OF TWO BURGHS

the archaeology of Old and New Aberdeen

SUPPORTED BY HISTORIC BUILDINGS AND MONUMENTS

AaE
1.
997081

Published by Aberdeen Art Gallery and Museums,
City of Aberdeen District Council © 1987

Edited by: J.A. Stones
Text: D.H. Evans, J.C. Murray, J.A. Stones
Photography: B.R. White
Design: J. Dunbar
Illustration: J. Dunbar

Printed in Edinburgh by Waddie & Co. Ltd.

ISBN 0-900017-20-1

Contents

1. Introduction

Often described as the oil capital of northern Europe, Aberdeen has always been one of Scotland's major cities. In fact, it consists of two ancient burghs, namely Old and New Aberdeen. The former was a religious centre which developed around the Cathedral of St Machar from the 12th century. It was created a free burgh of barony by James IV in 1498, and finally merged with the City of Aberdeen in 1891. Its other notable feature is the third oldest university in Scotland, founded in 1495. In contrast, New Aberdeen was a thriving trading port, serving a rich hinterland. It was first granted status as a royal burgh during the reign of David I (1124-53), and by the 14th century it had grown to be pre-eminent amongst Scottish towns in terms of international trade.

Most of this book is concerned with the archaeology of New Aberdeen, but where appropriate, features of Old Aberdeen have been included to complement our understanding of the development of the two burghs. Although much is known from historical sources of the growth and development of New Aberdeen, very few tangible remains of the medieval town exist. This is in sharp contrast to some English cities (e.g. York) where whole streets lined with medieval buildings still survive.

Although little of medieval date survives above the ground, Aberdeen does in fact have a very rich archaeological heritage beneath it. The increased pace of inner city redevelopment in the early 1970s threatened this with destruction. Since 1973, rescue excavations have been carried out on a wide range of sites prior to rebuilding, and archaeologists from Aberdeen Art Gallery and Museums Department continue to monitor and excavate threatened sites and buildings. This book presents our conclusions after the first 13 years of rescue archaeology and research in the city.

1   1. *Aberdeen looking west from St Nicholas House.*

1

2. Excavating the city

In 1973, the extension of the Town House along the east frontage of Broad Street led to the discovery that Aberdeen was rich in archaeological remains. Since then all development within the city centre has been monitored. Where building work has shown that extensive archaeological deposits survive, excavations have subsequently taken place (fig 3). In this way we are continuing to build up a composite picture of the development of the city.

Selecting a site

Sometimes the presence of an important site is revealed by building work, but on other occasions we have to rely on different sources of information in choosing a site. One obvious source is old maps. The general layout of medieval Aberdeen can be conjectured from the map of the city drawn by Parson James Gordon of Rothiemay in 1661 (fig 4). Although not entirely accurate, Parson Gordon's map gives a reasonable impression of what Aberdeen looked like before large-scale modern expansion took place. It also shows the location of certain important landmarks of the medieval burgh, some of which, such as St Nicholas' Church, still exist, while others, such as the friaries or mills, have long disappeared. Later maps show where street alignments have changed or have remained over the centuries, or pin-point the dates at which features of the medieval burgh ceased to exist. Other forms of documentary evidence range from the wealth of material in the city archives to relatively modern newspaper reports. Aberdeen possesses the most complete set of town records in Scotland and it is sometimes possible to trace the history of individual properties, their boundaries and ownership. Chance finds of archaeological interest often hit the newspaper headlines in the 19th century, and observations made then can be useful in determining where to excavate now. For example, a number of finds of human skeletons in the Carmelite Street area of the Green in the 1890s and early 1900s helped to locate the position of the Carmelite Friary and indicated that a site at 12 Martin's Lane was worth excavating. Street names are often useful tools for establishing the historical associations of an area. Carmelite Street and Lane were named in the late 18th century when they were laid out across part of what had been the gardens of the Carmelite Friary. In the same way, Trinity Street and Trinity Lane may represent part of the boundaries of the house of the Trinitarian Friars.

The archaeologist is always dependent on the co-operation of other authorities. The Department of Planning and Building Control of Aberdeen District Council has always provided assistance through the insertion of archaeological conditions into planning agreements. Gas and water authorities, whose work frequently requires excavation, can draw attention to discoveries which they have made in the course of their

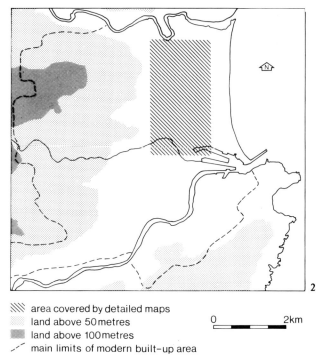

▨ area covered by detailed maps
▨ land above 50 metres
▨ land above 100 metres
⟋ main limits of modern built-up area

0   2km

2. *The area covered by the modern city of Aberdeen in relation to the area enclosed by its two ancient burghs.*

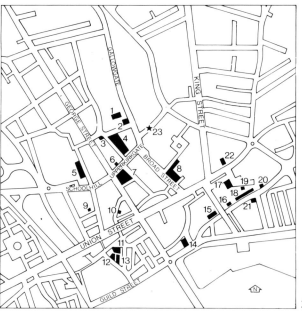

3. *The modern city centre, showing the sites excavated in New Aberdeen, together with the watching briefs mentioned in the text:* 1. *53-59 Gallowgate* 2. *45-47 Gallowgate* 3. *42 Loch St* 4. *42 St Paul St* 5. *2-16 Harriet St* 6. *42 Upper Kirkgate* 7. *43-57 Upper Kirkgate* 8. *12-26 Broad St, and 2-28 Queen St* 9. *6 Little Belmont St* 10. *13 Correction Wynd* 11. *45-59 Green* 12. *67-71 Green* 13. *12 Martin's Lane* 14. *Shore Brae* 15. *Virginia St, No. 3 Bonded Warehouse* 16. *17 Virginia St* 17. *6-8 Castle Terrace* 18. *21-37 Virginia St* 19. *Rear of 37 Virginia St* 20. *Virginia St steps, Castle Lane* 21. *42 Virginia St* 22. *Albion Court, 18 Castle St* 23. *British Telecom trenches in Littlejohn St (watching-brief).*

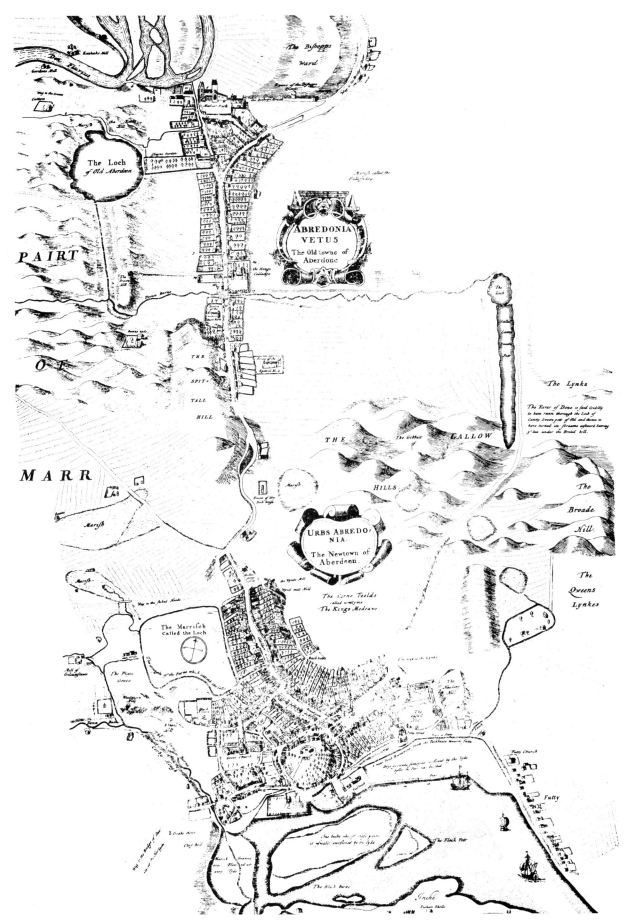

4. *Old and New Aberdeen in 1661, as depicted by Parson James Gordon of Rothiemay.*

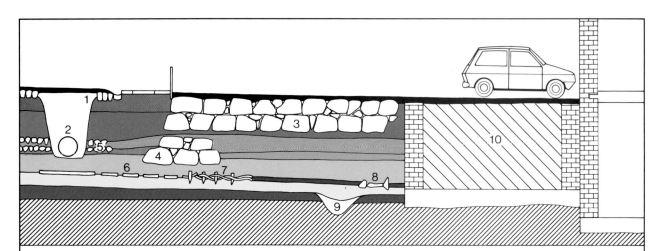

Key to features and layers

Features:

1. 19th-century cobbled road, cut away when sewer was laid during the 20th century.
2. 20th century sewer trench.
3. Stone foundations of 19th-century building, levelled to make car park.
4. Stone foundations of 15th-century building.
5. Successive layers of cobbles forming pathway in use from the 15th to the 19th century.
6. Pathway of wooden planks laid in the 14th century.
7. Foundations of 14th-century wattle-and-daub building.
8. Stones forming hearth inside building 7.
9. Rubbish pit dug into pre-1300 garden soil.
10. Rubble-filled cellar of recently demolished building.

Layers:

■ Modern tarmacadam road and pavement surfaces.
▨ Earth and sand brought in to raise ground level during 19th-century development.
▨ Soil accumulated over a period of disuse after demolition of building 4.
▨ Floor of building 4.
▨ Base for cobbled pathway 5.
□ Clay foundation for building 4.
■ Floor of building 7.
□ Layer of sand and gravel used as a base for path 6 and building 7.
▨ Original topsoil and ground level before first development around 1300.
▨ Undisturbed sandy subsoil.

5

work. Even apparently unpromising and unrelated disturbance of the ground can produce conspicuous archaeological evidence. For example, the observations of a narrow trench dug by British Telecom in Littlejohn Street in 1979 revealed traces of the easternmost edge of the medieval burgh at the point where layers of medieval refuse and occupation debris ended and marshland began.

Excavation is expensive and the provision of funds is a vital consideration. In Aberdeen the importance of the medieval burgh and the quality of its archaeological remains have long been recognised by Historic Buildings and Monuments, which has financed excavation over more than a decade.

The development of archaeological deposits

Modern machinery and large-scale re-development have increased the destructive capacity of foundations, as modern building often involves the removal of all soil down to the level of the subsoil. This process displaces all the intervening archaeological deposits. Before the 19th century, however, renewal of buildings necessitated only the demolition and levelling of foundations to provide an adequate surface for rebuilding. Sometimes a new structure would partially follow the lines of an old one, particularly in crowded urban communities where boundaries between properties, once established, did not greatly change for centuries. As a succession of buildings was constructed on the same

6

5. *The development of archaeological deposits.*

6. *An archaeological excavation gets under way on a site in the Gallowgate. Under the rubble of the demolished buildings earlier features, for example, the area of cobbling in the centre foreground, can be seen.*

7A

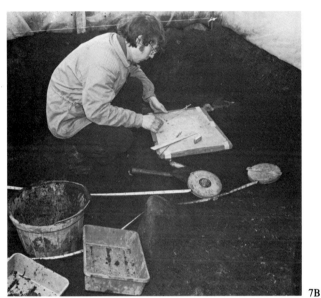

7B

8

plot over the centuries, an accumulation of layers representing all these activities was established (fig 5). Reconstruction of the use of a particular piece of land throughout its history can be suggested from the excavation and careful recording of these layers by photography and drawings.

Excavation

This is always undertaken to a strict time limit and trenches are sited to answer specific questions. Where possible, it is always better to examine the area of a site nearest to the street frontage. This would always have been the first part of the plot to be developed, would have reflected all the changes of later land use and would have supported the most substantial buildings. Nevertheless, the areas behind the frontage, known as backlands, can produce much useful information about the occupation and later development of these plots.

An excavation begins with demolition of standing buildings and the removal of the uppermost layers of rubble and topsoil; sometimes machinery may be used. This allows us to uncover areas in which archaeological deposits lie (fig 6).

Excavation is a destructive process, and if we are to destroy a site we must make a full and accurate record of what is there. As excavation progresses, the various layers and features such as pits, ditches and wall foundations, together with their contents, are described and recorded in detail on plans and in photographs (fig 7). Each layer is numbered and it is drawn and described in relation to all the other layers which surround it. From this basic record an interpretation is formed of what has happened on the site over the centuries, for example, was a group of pits used for the storage of perishable goods, or for the disposal of rubbish or cess? (fig 8). Quite often only tenuous remains are found – a row of stakes intertwined with wattles and branches may represent the wall of a house, while a patch of sand may be its floor (fig 9).

After excavation

Once the excavation is completed, the archaeologist is left not only with a large archive in the form of plans, notebooks and photographs, but also with a large number of finds – pottery, animal bones, pieces of iron and other metals and remains of wooden and other organic objects, some of which are very fragile. Examination of all this evidence often takes several months or years, but will eventually produce a reasoned analysis of a site out of a jumble of disparate walls, pits, postholes and middens. This work is done predominantly by archaeologists here in Aberdeen, in

7. *On each site a detailed record is maintained by drawing plans, photography and surveying.*

8. *A medieval storage pit. The wattle hurdle used as a cover has collapsed into the pit. St Paul Street, 14th century.*

9

consultation with specialists from other parts of Britain and even Europe. For example, an enigmatic feature excavated at St Paul Street was eventually identified as a bread oven, because of its similarity to one excavated at Aarhus in Denmark (fig 10).

One of our prime concerns is to establish the dates at which different buildings were constructed and people lived and worked on a site. One way in which this can be done is by examining the objects found in the course of the excavation. A coin in the right context, for example embedded in a wall foundation, may help to date the construction of that wall to within a very short time span, perhaps of 10 years or so. Fragments of clay tobacco pipes, in everyday use in the 17th-19th centuries, can allow a feature to be dated within 20 years. However, in the majority of cases we rely on pottery for our dating evidence. Usually this can allow us to date a feature to within a century or so on the basis of its shape, style of decoration and place of manufacture.

Radio-carbon dating has also been successfully used in Aberdeen. This method has been used to date the group of skeletons found during the excavation of the Carmelite Friary to within 100 years, showing that burials were taking place at this site for some 225 years

10A

9. *Foundations of 14th-century post-and-wattle building, St Paul Street.*

10. *The base of a bread oven as it appeared during excavation at 42 St Paul Street (A). The superstructure of the oven would have comprised a dome-shaped wattle frame covered with daub or clay (B). A fire would have been lit inside, the smoke escaping through the upper hole. Once the heat required for baking was achieved, the ashes would have been raked out and the bread put in to cook.*

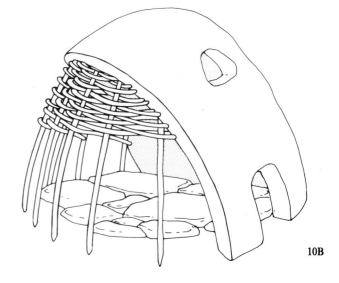

10B

from the late 14th century, and continued after the Reformation.

The objects recovered during excavation are not only of interest in dating the site; they also help to fill in the picture of how people lived and worked in the town. They can produce evidence of crafts and industries, of fittings of houses and buildings, of clothing and food and cooking. Residues found in cesspits provide information about diet, while the health and stature of individuals can be assessed by examination of their skeletons. Some of the more exotic finds can shed some light on the far-flung trading links of the community.

When our study of this material is completed, the results are made available for publication on several different levels, ranging from publications such as this, to highly specialised reports for other archaeologists. The best of the finds are displayed in local museums, but the bulk of the material will remain in store for the benefit of future research.

12. *Culter paper mill, which closed down in 1981.*

11. *42 Upper Kirkgate being observed during a recent major rebuilding: the front wall of this listed building was found to be leaning dangerously into the street, and had to be completely dismantled and rebuilt – a process which gave us a rare opportunity to record many of the details of its construction, which would normally be hidden behind panelling or lath and plaster-work on the inside of the building, and rendering on the outside. Originally built in about 1680, it is one of the few buildings of this date left in New Aberdeen which have their gable ends facing on to the street.*

7

Recording standing buildings and vanishing industries

As we have seen, very few buildings earlier than 1700 survive in the city. In recent years opportunities have arisen to survey a selection of 17th and 18th-century structures before alteration or demolition – for example, the recording of a group of cottages at Albion Court off Castlegate, or the frontage of 42 Upper Kirkgate before its reconstruction (fig 11). In addition, where 16th and 17th-century buildings were demolished during the last 100 years, photographs and drawings can sometimes survive to complement our picture of buildings in the city.

Efforts are being made to record the more recent architectural heritage of the Church in Aberdeen, where, as elsewhere, falling congregations and amalgamations have placed the future of many churches in jeopardy. Archaeologists have been responsible for recording the interiors and exteriors of churches – as well as salvaging some distinctive furnishings and stained glass before such events occur, for example at the former St Paul's Episcopal Church, built off Gallowgate in 1867 and demolished in 1986.

Another area of interest is the recording and salvaging of Aberdeen's rapidly disappearing industries and commercial enterprises, ranging from buildings and machinery of the now almost defunct granite industry, to relatively small-scale industries such as pipe or brick-making (fig 12). A recent study of this sort was the photographic recording of Kettock's Mill, one of the oldest meal mills on the River Don, prior to its conversion into flats. Other recent projects have included the collection of some of the furnishings and equipment of a local chemist's shop, while a survey of 18th and 19th-century funeral monuments is in progress.

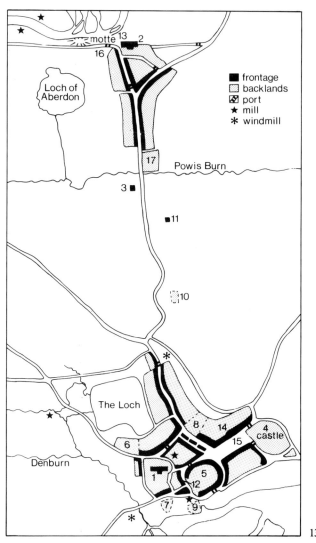

13

13. *Old and New Aberdeen during the Middle Ages, with the main buildings mentioned in the text. THE CHURCHES: 1. St Nicholas' 2. St Machar's 3. St Mary of the Snows 4. St Ninian's Chapel 5. St Katherine's Chapel THE RELIGIOUS HOUSES: 6. The Blackfriars 7. The Carmelites 8. The Greyfriars 9. The Trinitarians THE HOSPITALS: 10. The Leper Hospital, Spital Hill 11. St Peter's Hospital 12. St Thomas the Martyr's Hospital 13. St Mary's Hospital PUBLIC BUILDINGS AND INSTITUTIONS: 14. The Tolbooth 15. Flesh and Fish markets in Castle Street 16. Old Market Stance in Old Aberdeen 17. King's College.*

14. *Tillydrone Motte in Seaton Park.*

14

8

15

16

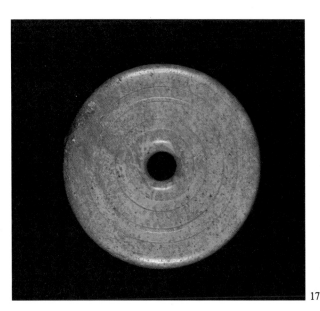

17

3. Life in the medieval town

Town layout

The present-day appearance of Aberdeen is dominated by the early 19th-century construction of the long, straight thoroughfares of Union Street, King Street and George Street, which have entirely flattened the dramatically hilly landscape within which the medieval city nestled. Parson Gordon wrote in the commentary to his map of 1661, 'In our age the most considerable part of the city standeth on three hills – the Castle Hill, St Katherine's Hill and the Gallowgate Hill. The city itself is situated betwixt these three – or at least the best part of it – the swelling of those hills is hardly discerned by such as walk along the streets, yet their height is apparent to those who dwell in the suburbs or without the town.' Such was the burgh in the 17th century, but what did it look like in the medieval period? The town grew up around a natural harbour and was sited on the focus of the main roads leading to and from that anchorage. Its street pattern was dominated by two main streets at right-angles to one another: Broad Street/Gallowgate formed the main route from Old Aberdeen and the north, whilst Castle Street formed part of the road to the south and also served as a link between the castle at one end of the burgh and the parish church at the other. A number of other streets radiated from this basic outline, among them Upper and Nether Kirkgate, Shore Brae, Futty Wynd, Putachie Wynd, and all of these can be shown to be in existence by the year 1300. The medieval market place lay at the centre of the town in Castle Street, where the flesh and fish crosses were sited: it is possible that a second and earlier market may have existed in Broad Street, but later passed out of use and was covered with houses (fig 13).

The east end of the settlement was dominated by the Castle Hill, and a castle certainly existed here by 1264. The original date of its construction is obscure, but the importance of its position next to a royal burgh suggests a royal foundation. As the site was almost totally destroyed in the 1960s, we have had no opportunity to determine any details of its form or the nature of its construction. At the west end of the settlement, stands the Parish Church of St Nicholas, which was originally built in the 12th century.

Aberdeen, in common with most Scottish towns, was not walled, and no evidence of defensive ditches has been found, but there would appear to have been a considerable degree of natural defence, such as the Loch and various stretches of marshy ground. By the later Middle Ages, a system of ports or gates straddled the main thoroughfares into the town. These served to control the flow of goods into the market and could be

15. *Aberdeen's main trading links during the Middle Ages.*

16. *A grey-ware pitcher from the Low Countries. It holds a little over 13 litres (about 23 pints – almost 3 gallons!). Gallowgate, late 14th century.*

17. *A decorated spindle whorl, lathe-turned from a piece of elephant tusk. Queen Street, 13th-14th century.*

closed at time of curfew. The last of these ports was removed in 1769 and we have no idea what they looked like.

To the south-west lay the area known as the Green. Various previous writers have suggested that this was the original focus of settlement, but this claim can be questioned. Much of the basis of the claim rests on two arguments. The first relies on a 16th-century story that King William the Lion had a palace here. This legend may have originated from attempts by the Trinitarian Friars to claim a royal origin for their house (allegedly this palace was handed over to them by the King) and has no basis in fact. The second argument centres around the position of St Nicholas' Church apparently outside the main area of settlement enclosed by the ports or gates, but this hinges upon the ports being part of the original plan, whereas in fact they may be a secondary feature.

In Old Aberdeen, the focus of settlement was on a rectangle represented today by the Chanonry and Don Street. It was bounded on the north by St Machar's Cathedral and to the east by Chaplain's Court and the Bishop's Palace. The burgh lay on the line of the major land routes to north, south and west. The road to the west ran past Tillydrone Motte (fig 14). This is a small example of the earliest form of castle to be found in the region. These consisted of an artificial mound, topped by some sort of palisade, which enclosed one or more timber buildings, and date from the 12th century. Larger and better examples can still be seen at Inverurie and Duffus. The road to the north ran via the Bridge of Balgownie towards Ellon and other north-east burghs and ports. The High Street formed part of the road to the south. Parson Gordon's map shows ribbon development extending much further to the south along the road to New Aberdeen, but the fact that King's College could be established in such a large area of open land as late as 1495, and also that several other churches and hospitals were sited further south along this route, would suggest that much of the present College Bounds and the Spital was largely a development of the 17th and 18th centuries. To some extent this is borne out by the siting of the Market Cross at the north end of the High Street, near the position of the present Town House. As with New Aberdeen, this settlement was also bounded by a number of ports, none of which survive today.

Aberdeen's trading links

Situated at the mouth of the River Dee on a fine natural harbour, Aberdeen was ideally placed to serve as a market for the surrounding rural areas. This is reflected

18

19

20

18. *The upper part of a jug made in Scarborough, Yorkshire. It is vividly decorated with a representation of a human figure – the face begins just below the rim, and the two hands can be seen just above the waist, clutching the base of a long flowing beard. Broad Street, 13th-14th century.*

19. *The copper-alloy cauldron which contained the Upper Kirkgate hoard of over 12,000 silver coins, hidden in about 1336. Vessels like these were used in most households for boiling and stewing over open fires.*

20. *A locally-made pottery jug, found by workmen during the construction of the St Nicholas Centre in 1983. It contained somewhere in the region of 3,000 silver pennies dating from the late 13th and early 14th centuries, the impressions of which can clearly be seen on the inside of the vessel.*

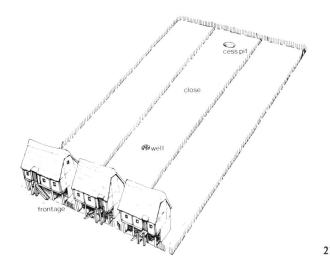

close

cess pit

well

frontage

21

22

in its main exports, which were wool, hides, skins, salmon, tallow and other animal products. Most of this trade was with ports in present-day Belgium and Holland (fig 15). On the trip home, the boats brought back luxuries and manufactured goods such as wine, books, drugs and spices, clothing, precious objects in gold, silver and enamel, glass and weapons. Another important link was with the Baltic and in particular the major port of Danzig. This supplied timber, lint, wax, grain, iron and amber. Most of this trade is not represented in the archaeological record because it consisted of perishable goods. However, occasionally some confirmation of this trade is found in pottery and other objects. The range of pottery vessels present in the city includes examples from the Rhineland, northern Holland and Belgium, France and Spain (figs 15, 16). A piece of Italian silk and an elephant ivory spindle-whorl (fig 17), presumably from Africa, point to wider links. But another important trade is represented by coastal connections with the ports of eastern England, and this is illustrated by large quantities of pottery from Yorkshire and Lincolnshire and smaller quantities from East Anglia and London (fig 18).

Considering the wealth of the burgh and the volume of trade which is documented in its records, very little money seems to have been in everyday circulation; in 13 years of extensive excavation, remarkably few individual coins have been found. In contrast, somewhere in the region of 50,000 coins have been found in eight medieval coin hoards in or around the edges of the medieval burgh. Of these only three survive. The Upper Kirkgate hoard, found in 1886, consisted of about 12,000 coins buried in a bronze pot (fig 19). Another two hoards have been found in the last couple of years and contain some 7,000 coins buried in two pottery jars (fig 20). All three hoards were composed mainly of silver pennies of the reigns of Edward I (1272-1307) and Edward II (1307-27) of England together with a few coins of Scotland, Ireland and the Continent. This is very characteristic of coin hoards of this period, as most coinage in circulation was from English mints. Before the advent of banking, burying your money was the usual way of keeping it safe. The only unusual aspect of these hoards is that so many of them were never reclaimed by their owners, which might suggest that some, at least, were concealed during a period when Aberdeen was caught up in warfare during the campaigns of Edward III in the 1330s.

21. *The layout of a typical medieval tenement. The main building was on the street frontage, and often consisted of a shop or booth on the ground floor with accommodation above; access to the upper floors may often have been by an external staircase. Each building would have backed on to a close, in which its well and cess pit would have been sited; some of the closes would also have boasted the occasional shed or outhouse, but mostly they were used for tending stock, or as kitchen gardens. By the later Middle Ages this pattern of use was changing, and people were beginning to build houses in what were to become the 'backlands'.*

22. *A 13th-century timber sill beam excavated in the Gallowgate: a wall of planks or wattle uprights would have been set in the groove running down the centre of the beam. The low stone foundation beneath it would have given the building stability, and acted as a sort of primitive damp course – thereby extending the life of the timber.*

Medieval houses and shops

The medieval town was divided into numerous long and narrow plots, called 'rigs', which extended back behind the houses on the street frontage (fig 21). At the beginning of this period, all of these houses were probably built parallel to the street – though at a later date, some buildings would be placed at right-angles to the frontages, in order to fit more houses into the same amount of space. Some of the more important people in the town, such as the wealthier merchants and burgesses, were to own and occupy whole buildings; but houses were also split into flats, and most people lived in rented rooms. A common practice was to have a shop on the ground floor, with residential accommodation on the upper floors. The inhabitants of the medieval burgh included a whole host of craftsmen, who needed small workshops. Goldsmiths, cobblers, cutlers, spinners and weavers could carry on their work in the backrooms and attics of ordinary houses: some may even have sold their wares from the shops or booths, which opened directly on to the street. When a building was split into two or more flats, these were often served by separate entrances from the street – sometimes with an external staircase (or 'forestair') leading to the upper floors. A passage or 'pend' ran through or alongside the building into a 'close'.

We have no real idea of the size of the town in the year 1200, but we think that its population in the early 15th century was somewhere between 2,500 and 3,000. The physical limits of the burgh were dictated by the surrounding natural features, such as hills, rivers, lochs and marshes; so the demand for housing space within the town increased as its population grew. One of the ways to fit more people into the same amount of space was to build houses at right-angles to the street (a number of 18th-century examples of buildings with their gables facing on to the street can still be seen in the High Street in Old Aberdeen). Another way was just to make the buildings higher, by adding extra floors, and thus more rooms per house. A third answer was to start building houses within the old 'closes', which from now on were to be known as the 'backlands'. All three of these methods of coping with an expanding population were tried in Aberdeen during the later Middle Ages, with the result that there was a steady growth both in the amount of rented accommodation available, and in property speculation: in fact, by the middle of the 15th century, over a third of the property changing hands within the town belonged to the top 11 families. The highest rents were to be found in the fashionable streets, such as the Castlegate, the Gallowgate and Exchequer Row; whilst much lower rents were to be had in the Upper and Nether Kirkgates, and the cheapest of all were to be found in the Green. Another result of the growth in size and prosperity of the burgh was that it became both convenient and fashionable for many of the rural lords to buy or build their own 'town houses', in which to stay when they came here on business; hence, important families such as the Earls of Errol, Mar

23A

23. *A tiled roof consisted mostly of flat tiles which were carefully overlapped; each tile was secured to the wooden boards (or 'sarking') underneath by a pair of nails which passed through holes in its top corners. The tops of the ridges were covered with pottery ridge tiles (A), which were often elaborately moulded and decorated, and covered in shiny yellow, green or brown glazes. Occasionally, one or even both ends of the ridge might be capped by a finial in the shape of a spinning-top (B), or less commonly, of an intricately carved human head or an exotic animal.*

and Buchan were to acquire large properties on the more desirable streets such as the Castlegate and the Gallowgate.

Up until now, we have not been able to excavate many of the buildings on the street frontages, because it is precisely these areas which have usually been most heavily disturbed by the deep cellars of 18th and 19th-century buildings. Nevertheless, we can make some shrewd guesses about the shape of these buildings and what form they took. As well as the churches and the castle, a handful of stone buildings probably existed in the two medieval burghs – for example, a court case of 1317 mentions a stone house on the Gallowgate; but these would always have been the exceptions. The majority of the bigger houses would have been built around timber frames, with wattle-and-daub walling; whilst some of the smaller houses may have had wattle walls supported by freestanding posts. The foundations of both types of building were sometimes laid on low stone walls, and sometimes on large wooden beams (fig 22); examples of both have been found in recent excavations in the Gallowgate. Some of the bigger buildings had roofs covered with gaily coloured pottery tiles (fig 23) - occasionally finished with elaborately decorated finials, such as found on a site in St Paul Street. Some of the other buildings by the end of this

24. *A reconstruction of a 'backland' site such as that excavated on St Paul Street. In the late 13th and early 14th centuries a number of post-and-wattle buildings were standing on these tenements. Some of the rigs were surrounded by wattle fences; others were separated from one another by boundary ditches. At least one of the properties had a large bread oven in the close, and here we see a baker unloading a batch from his oven.*

period had slate roofs; yet, by far the majority would have been thatched with heather, rushes or straw.

The bulk of our evidence for buildings comes from sites in the backlands where quite a few post-and-wattle buildings have now been excavated. All of these were built at right-angles to the street frontage – i.e. on the same alignment as the rigs themselves. Some of the best preserved examples were found on the St Paul Street site, and range in date from the later 12th to the mid-14th century (fig 24). One such structure measured nearly 4m wide, and was about 7 or 8m long, and had wattle walls built around freestanding upright posts. These walls may have been lined with mud or dung or may even have been strengthened with a layer of turves stacked against the outside. The roofs would probably have been thatched, with a hole at one end to let out the smoke. The doorways were set in the side walls, and would have been closed with a wattle or plank door. Windows, where they existed, consisted of little more than a small lined opening in the wall, which would be shuttered or covered with straw matting at night and in bad weather; additional lighting would have been given by candles (made from sheep's fat) or oil lamps (small pottery or stone basins filled with olive or rape-seed oil, and fuelled by a rush wick).

Small stone hearths have been found in the middle of the floors of some of these buildings. Where such hearths are not associated with industrial slags and residues, we are probably safe in assuming that we

are dealing with houses; but others may have been workshops, or buildings for housing stock of one sort or another; whilst some of the smaller ones were clearly little more than sheds. This sort of picture would seem to be confirmed by the 1434 grant which refers to 'permission to build a house of two bays' (on the frontage), 'with *outhouses* behind'. The floors of the excavated buildings consisted of clay or gravel surfaces, which would have originally been covered with straw. In some cases, differences in the floors between one end of the building and the other show that there were originally two rooms separated by an internal partition which no longer survives (e.g. a wattle hurdle): here, we may be dealing with a living-room at one end, with a work-room or a byre (for animals) at the other. We have already mentioned the demand for craft workshops in the medieval burgh, but there was also a great need for buildings in which to house stock. Many of the richer burgesses would have had their own ponies, which would have to be stabled, and many families kept pigs, sheep and hens (pigs and sheep were periodically let out to forage or graze on waste and open ground; in fact, pigs seem to have been a continual source of nuisance in the town up until the second half of the 19th century, with their continual rooting amongst the middens, and people building styes for them in the streets themselves). The rigs were clearly defined by boundary ditches and wattle fences. Many were sub-divided by wattle hurdles into a number of enclosures; this suggests that part of the plot was still being used as a kitchen garden, whilst other parts may have been used for penning animals. One of the persistent problems in the town was what to do with the rubbish. Food remains, household and animal muck, and the waste and residues from the various crafts, all had to be regularly disposed of – some of it went on to large communal tips or middens, such as once existed in Queen Street; some was cast into the streets; some was piled up in small middens in the rigs themselves; whilst much of the rest was used to infill old quarries and pits, which had originally been dug for sand and gravel for building; occasionally, it was put into purpose-dug cesspits, which would be periodically cleaned out. Ultimately, most of this rubbish ended up on the town fields and crofts, as manure, but usually not before it had lain around the rigs, in one form or another.

Another prominent feature within the rigs was the well or water-butt. As the town grew larger, the demand for water increased – particularly during the drier months of the summer. This demand came not only from individual households, but also from the many industries; for example, the millers needed it to drive their mills, the fullers, dyers and tanners to soak their products, the smiths for quenching their products, and the brewers for making ale. So, the Loch, and the burns and springs flowing through the town were used by all and sundry, and, as time went by, became quite polluted in some stretches. Large communal wells were sited in major streets such as the Castlegate, where copious supplies of water were also needed to wash away the waste from the meat and fish markets which were held there. In addition to these, most households would have had access to a well sunk in the close, and many others would have had water-butts (large open barrels set upright to collect rain water); the remains of a number of such barrels were found on the St Paul Street site.

Medieval churches and religious buildings

In the Middle Ages, many of the most imposing buildings in a town were associated with the Church. It is difficult in late 20th-century Britain to visualize the importance and influence of the Church in the medieval period. Not only was it one of the wealthiest institutions in urban and rural life; it was also a dominant influence on people's lives, occupying many roles now assumed by the state, such as education and the social services, as

25

26

25. *St Machar's Cathedral, Old Aberdeen, founded in the 12th century. The cathedral today comprises the nave of the church as it was rebuilt in the 15th century. This view shows the blocked east gable where, up until the 17th century, the transepts and choir would have stood.*

26. *Interior of St Machar's Cathedral, looking towards the east end of the 15th-century nave.*

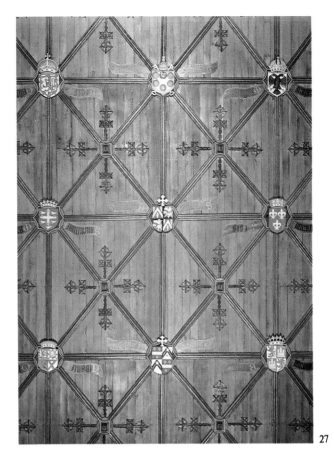

27

28

well as fulfilling spiritual needs. Further, it was a world in which the place of man in the universe and his relationship with God as creator was unquestioned. The significant role played by the Parish Church of St Nicholas even in the mid-17th century is suggested by the exaggerated size given to it on Parson Gordon's map. Religion provided hope in a transitory and painful life, and the Church received considerable benefits from donors who thought by a gift to reduce the time spent by themselves or their loved ones in recompense for their sins in life. By the close of the 14th century, the two burghs had a cathedral, St Machar's, at Old Aberdeen, a parish church, St Nicholas', two houses of friars (the Carmelites and the Dominicans), one house of canons (Trinitarians), a leper hospital, and a hospital, St Peter's, Old Aberdeen. Most of these religious institutions would have stood out as stone buildings among the predominantly timber dwellings of the town. But today, with the exception of the Drum and Collison aisles at St Nicholas', which may in part date to the late 12th or early 13th centuries, and portions of the east end of St Machar's Cathedral, there are no visible remains of the Church in either centre prior to the year 1400.

Cathedral

We do not know precisely when the first church was built in Aberdeen. The bishopric was established about the year 1130, and the first cathedral seems to have been built within 30 years of that date. Legend suggests that the site of the cathedral was first used for the establishment of a Celtic monastery in the 6th century by St Machar but there is no positive evidence for that claim. Any church of that date would probably have been a timber building and any traces of it have long disappeared beneath later development on the site. The cathedral served a diocese covering Aberdeenshire and Buchan, and by the Reformation had 100 parishes. St Machar's as we see it today comprises the nave of the building broadly as it was rebuilt during the 15th century (fig 25). To the east stood the transepts and choir, which have been in ruins since the 17th century and may never in fact have been absolutely complete. In the Middle Ages the cathedral lay at the centre of a bustling 'close' and the modern street The Chanonry defines the area occupied by the canons or priests and other officials of the cathedral. At one time St Machar's had a chapter of 30 canons drawn from the various parishes within the diocese.

The appearance of the cathedral's interior today largely reflects the way in which it was restored during the 19th century (fig 26). In the Middle Ages it would have been much more colourful, with painted plaster on the walls and pillars of the nave, complementing the impressive heraldic ceiling (fig 27). A screen of wood or stone separated the choir, where the canons held their services, from the nave where the general public would have worshipped. The serried ranks of wooden pews are

27. 16th-century heraldic ceiling at St Machar's. The three rows of shields contain, left, the arms of the noble families of Scotland, headed by King James V, middle, the arms of the Scottish prelates and, right, the arms of the sovereigns of Europe.

28. 19th-century photograph of St Nicholas' Church, showing the 15th-century oak steeple which was destroyed by fire in 1874.

29

30

29. *St Mary's Chapel, beneath the east end of St Nicholas' Church, was built in the 15th century as a mortuary chapel for the powerful Gordon family.*
30. *St Fittick's Church and churchyard, Nigg Bay.*

31A

31B

31C

31. Marginal roundels from a French Book of Hours, about 1470, showing Carmelite (A), Franciscan (B) and Dominican (C) friars.

a relatively modern arrangement: in medieval times, seating would not have been provided, except perhaps for a stone bench around the wall, but within the nave would have stood a number of altars, in many cases set up by benefactors for the future good of their souls.

Parish churches

The origins of the Parish Church of St Nicholas are almost as old as the burgh itself (fig 28). It is first mentioned in a Papal Bull of 1157, but very little survives of the building of that period. Excavations within the church in 1974 suggested that part of the crossing may indeed be as early as the mid-12th century. Parson Gordon gives a detailed description of a church which he claims was constructed in 1060, but there is no independent evidence to suggest that Aberdeen was sufficiently developed to have had a parish church at that date. Neither do we know on what authority Gordon based his claim. As befits the main church of an important burgh, St Nicholas' has been greatly changed over the centuries. A survival of the 15th-century church is the chapel of St Mary, built beneath the east end as a burial chapel for the powerful Gordon family (fig 29). Such mortuary or chantry chapels were a common feature of medieval churches, providing a means of perpetual prayer for the departed as well as a source of finance for the church. The present church of St Nicholas largely dates from the 18th and 19th centuries.

In the late 15th century, Old Aberdeen acquired a parish church, dedicated to St Mary of the Snows. The name recalls the legend that a 4th-century Pope was told by the Virgin Mary to found a church in Rome on a spot where snow fell in August. Little is known about the size or shape of Aberdeen's Snow Kirk, as the church itself was demolished in the 17th century. Its site is preserved as a Roman Catholic graveyard on the west side of College Bounds.

Other medieval churches in the Aberdeen area were built to serve specific purposes or groups of people. Long after the demise of the town's castle, in the 14th century, a chapel, dedicated to St Ninian, existed on the Castle Hill, and was still receiving endowments in the early 16th century. A chapel also existed on St Katherine's Hill, although its date of foundation is not known. At the nearby village of Footdee, St Clement's Church served the white fishers from the later 15th century, while the church of St Fittick at Nigg was provided for the outlying community to the south perhaps as early as the 12th century (fig 30).

Religious houses

Between the 13th and 15th centuries three groups of friars and one of canons were established in Aberdeen (fig 34). The friars were a development of European Christianity in the 13th century and played an important role in the 300 years prior to the Reformation. During the 13th century, they established houses all over Europe, often in cities and towns as centres of population, as they were committed to preaching the gospel to

17

ordinary people. Different orders of friars emphasised different aspects of the religious life, but many were noted as preachers, and the Dominicans (named after their Italian founder, St Dominic) acquired a reputation for learning, often possessing extensive libraries as well as schools. The Dominicans, also called Blackfriars (after the colour of their cloaks, worn over a white tunic), may have been the first friars to arrive in Aberdeen; their house was established some time after the year 1300 on the site now occupied by part of Robert Gordon's College and Aberdeen Art Gallery. We know little about the extent or layout of the buildings. Newspaper accounts of the finds made during building work between 1833 and 1923 suggest that the main complex (and the church) were located near to modern Blackfriars Street in about the position now occupied by the College gymnasium. A building discovered in 1833, sited 'about mid way between the street (Blackfriars?) and the hospital (Robert Gordon's)' was '60 feet long and faced the south', and may have been the church. A substantial stone-built grave, containing three bodies, may represent the burial of a benefactor and his family, within the church, while the main cemetery lay outside the church, possibly extending under the present Art Gallery. Part of what may have been the main drain and some lead piping from the water supply, were also found during these excavations.

We should expect a friary complex such as this to have included a series of residential and domestic buildings. These may have included a refectory, or dining room, a dormitory and a chapter house for discussing friary business. From the charter granting the land to the Earl Marischal of Scotland after the Reformation, we can infer that a barn, a kiln, a dovecot, a garden and an orchard were also included.

By the mid-14th century, the Carmelite or White Friars were settled in the burgh. Their name derives from groups of hermits of European nationality who lived around Mount Carmel in Palestine and were brought back by Crusaders in the mid-13th century. Relatively little is known about the lifestyle of this particular order of friars – in their early days they tended to maintain some aspects of their ascetic origins, establishing houses in relatively remote areas, but by the time they arrived in Aberdeen, their character seems to have been altered to conform with the other groups of mendicant, or begging friars. Apart from street names (Carmelite Street and Lane) in the Green and various finds of skeletons and a possible building during the 19th and early 20th centuries, until recently nothing was known of the site or the nature of this Aberdeen friary.

In 1981, an excavation at 12 Martin's Lane uncovered remains of the church, which may date to the 14th century (fig 32). This substantial stone buttressed building is quite in keeping with the functional needs of the friars' lifestyle. However, the church would not have been entirely undecorated, as is clear from the numerous fragments of painted and stained window glass which were found during the excavation (fig 33).

33

33. *Fragments of painted window glass. Carmelite Friary, 13th-14th century.*

18

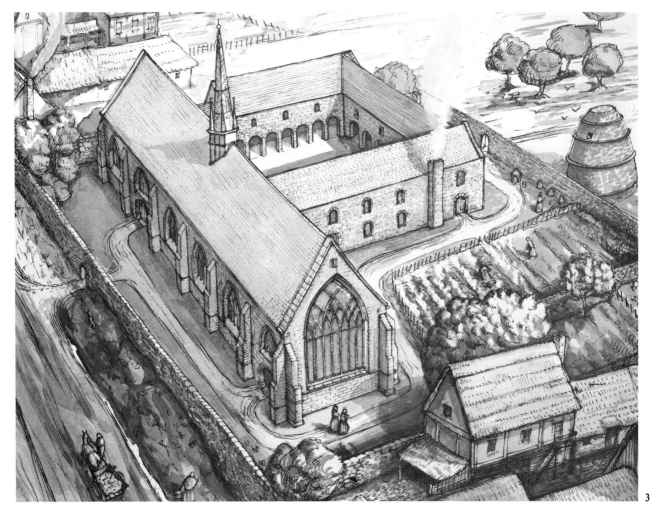

32. *The substantial foundations of the building thought to be the church of the Carmelite friars.*

34. *An impression of a typical Aberdeen friary before the Reformation. Adjoining the church are residential accommodation for the friars and their guests, a kitchen, brewhouse, bakehouse, a refectory and a library. Near the church there would also be a chapterhouse, where friary business would be conducted. In the wider area, gardens and orchards would have been cultivated by the friars or lay servants, while beehives and a dovecot provided other important sources of sustenance.*

35

36

35. *Greyfriars Church, built in the early 16th century, demolished in 1903 to make way for the new west front of Marischal College.*

36. *The old Aberdeen Trades' Hall, shown here during demolition, was built on the site of the Trinitarian Friary, and may well have incorporated some of the medieval friary buildings.*

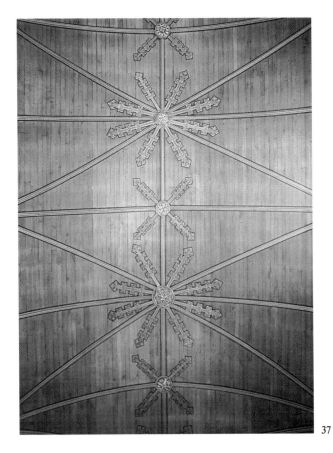

37

38

37. *Early 16th-century oak ceiling, King's College Chapel.*

38. *Pulpit in King's College Chapel. In the mid-16th century Bishop Stewart provided St Machar's with a new pulpit. After it went out of use in 1793 it lay in store for several years and finally many of the carved panels from it were used in this structure for King's College.*

Although much decayed, they give a general impression of the appearance of some of the windows. Small 'quarries' of glass were fitted into H-shaped strips of lead, some of which have also been found. Much of the decoration took the form of black or brown painted designs of leaves and fruit on plain white glass, although two pieces of glass, stained ruby red and aquamarine blue, give an indication that certain colours were also in use. Other features of the friary buildings revealed by the excavation included a number of stone slates from the roof (imported from a quarry in the Forfar area) and a portion of lead piping possibly from the friary water supply, which would have been relatively sophisticated compared with that of the town itself at the time.

In 1469, land was given to a group of observantine Franciscans (a reformed order of Greyfriars) to allow them to found a friary: some members of that order had already been at work in Aberdeen since about 1461. The site lay on the east side of Broad Street, in much the same area now occupied by Marischal College. We know nothing of their earliest church and domestic buildings, but in 1518-32 a new church was financed by Bishop Gavin Dunbar (fig 35). This survived in part until 1903, when it was removed to make way for the College's new west front. Photographs give something of the flavour of the building, and at the demolition the fine south window was painstakingly removed to be rebuilt as the west window of the new Greyfriars Church, where it can still be seen (fig 36). We are fortunate that there survives for this friary an obituary calendar giving names and very brief biographies of friars and benefactors. Many friars are simply described as 'priest, preacher and confessor' or 'specially devout and exemplary' but amongst them are also two carpenters, one of whom it is said constructed a belfry and cells for the friars, and a Friar John Strang who was both a priest and a glass worker, glazing the Franciscan churches of Perth, Elgin and Ayr, as well as the first Franciscan church at Aberdeen.

The Trinitarians, often called Redfriars (they are said to have worn a red cross on their habit) probably arrived in Aberdeen in the 13th century. They were not a mendicant, or begging, order, and were therefore not strictly speaking friars, but canons, living according to the rule of St Augustine. They were allowed to receive endowments, the incomes of which they used to support poor travellers or redeem captives from the infidels in the Holy Land.

There is a well-known tradition that King William the Lion gave his palace in the Green to the Trinitarians to found their friary, but this legend dates only from the 16th century and is extremely unlikely to be true. The friary church, which probably stood at the south end of what is now Exchange Street, was demolished in 1794, but some of the other buildings, given after the Reformation to the Incorporated Trades of the City, survived until the 1840s, when they were demolished to make way for Guild Street and the development of the railway. A photograph shows the Trades' Hall during demolition, and although it gives the appearance of a 17th-century structure, it may well have incorporated some of the medieval friary buildings (fig 36). According to an anonymous local antiquary, during the demolition, skeletons, a coffin, some structural timbers, pieces of jerkins and shoes were uncovered in what must have been extremely water-logged conditions, and we can only be disappointed that no archaeologists were present at that time.

Two other religious houses often said to have been sited in Aberdeen owe more to tradition than to fact. There is no documentary evidence for a convent of nuns on St Katherine's Hill, and the Knights Templar (a military order founded in 1118 to protect pilgrims after the capture of Jerusalem) did not have a house at the north-east corner of the Castlegate – they merely held land there.

Hospitals

During the medieval period the care of the sick, the poor and the elderly was a function of the Church. Hospitals were founded for the protection of different groups of afflicted people and often the founder was a bishop or cleric. The foundation of a leper hospital on the Spital Hill, first mentioned in 1333, was also no doubt the result of an instinct of self-preservation – an attempt to isolate the unclean at a relatively remote spot. Leprosy and other unpleasant skin diseases were regarded with such abhorrence that they were thought to pose a threat even after death. Lepers were probably buried in the

39. *Carved canopies of choir stalls, King's College Chapel.*

40. *Interior of King's College Chapel, looking west towards the choir stalls and the rood screen. The screen was originally further east, in line with the high-level doorway visible top left, which allowed students to gain access to the chapel direct from the college by a spiral staircase within the screen. In the Middle Ages, the rood screen housed the organ, and also a large rood or crucifix, two altars and three small pulpits for reading lessons and preaching the sermon.*

39

40

41. *The stone effigies of Sir Alexander Irvine, 4th laird of Drum and his wife, Lady Elizabeth Keith, in St Nicholas' Church.*

42. *Effigy of Walter Ydil, at St Machar's Cathedral.*

vicinity of the hospital itself to avoid contamination, and it is interesting that no case of leprosy was recorded among the 13th to 17th-century skeletons excavated at the Carmelite Friary. The other four hospitals in the Aberdeen area were intended for the relief of the poor and the infirm. The earliest foundation was that of St Peter, by Matthew, Bishop of Aberdeen from 1172-99. This continued in use until shortly before the Reformation and foundations of part of the chapel may still be traced in St Peter's Cemetery. St Thomas the Martyr's hospital was founded in the Nether Kirkgate near the east end of St Nicholas' Church in 1459. It is said that during house building in this area in 1902 parts of the garden and cemetery were uncovered, but this account has not been confirmed. The other hospitals were St Mary's, founded by Bishop Gavin Dunbar to the west of the cathedral burial ground, for the care of 12 old men, and St Anne's at Footdee, a house for poor women.

Furnishing and decoration

In medieval times the interiors of major Aberdeen churches would have been richly appointed. The inventories of the riches of St Nicholas' and St Machar's at the Reformation show astonishing wealth in gold and silver, jewelled chalices, cloth of gold vestments, crosses, basins, and censers. Sadly, virtually all these disappeared into private hands, despite the elaborate efforts made by the Town Council and the Bishop of Aberdeen to protect them from the Reformers. A few furnishings do survive, however, to give an impression of Aberdeen

43. *Interior of St Nicholas' Church, by Sir George Reid, about 1880, show-ing the crossing beneath the tower, and the Collison Aisle, originally the north transept of the medieval parish church. The architecture is largely 12th-century in date, although subject to later alterations such as the 16th-century traceried window in the north wall.*

pre-Reformation church interiors. In the National Museums of Scotland there is a fragment of the pre-Reformation oak choir stalls of St Nicholas' Church, carved by John Fendour around 1507-8. When the old East Church was demolished in 1835, much of the fine woodwork of St Nicholas' was reputedly sold and converted into household furniture. The Convenor's chair, given to the crafts or trades of Aberdeen by Matthew Guild about 1570, is said to have been partly constructed from some of this woodwork, salvaged by Guild after the Reformation. St Nicholas' also possessed an elegant oak roof similar to the contemporary early 16th-century one still extant at King's College Chapel (fig 38). Both these ceilings may be the work of the same man, possibly again John Fendour. But the great asset of King's College Chapel, the canopied choir stalls, may not be by Fendour; although like his work they show the influence of Flemish or French craftsmanship (fig 39). The rood screen is not in its original place but it gives an indication of the kind of screen which would have graced many medieval Aberdeen churches. Its purpose was to divide the east end of the church or choir from the lay people's nave. Often a stairway within the screen gave access to a loft, frequently occupied by a large crucifix, or as at King's College, by an organ. Probably the latest example of medieval woodwork in Aberdeen, and one of the finest, is the heraldic ceiling of St Machar's Cathedral, which reflects a hierarchical procession of the secular and ecclesiastical personages of Scotland at the time (fig 27).

A few examples survive of the stone effigies which decorated the tombs of distinguished individuals during the medieval period. In St Nicholas' Church are those of Sir Alexander Irvine, 4th Laird of Drum (died 1457) and his wife, Lady Elizabeth Keith (fig 41). A fine effigy at St Machar's Cathedral commemorates Walter Ydil, one of the canons of the cathedral, and the prebendary of Deer, who died about 1472 (fig 42). It is particularly notable for the detail of the vestments he is wearing, including a fox-fur almuce or hood pulled up over his head – perhaps an indication of the chilly conditions prevalent at St Machar's in the Middle Ages.

Working lives and private lives

Burgh society encompassed all walks of life, from wealthy merchants, through skilled craftsmen to relatively poor unskilled labourers. As we have already seen from the exports of the port of Aberdeen, industries and crafts associated with the processing of animal products such as wool and leather, and the manufacture of goods from such raw materials, formed the basis of its wealth. Leather workers, tanners, skinners, cordiners, cobblers, saddlers, glovers, weavers, spinners and tailors formed

43

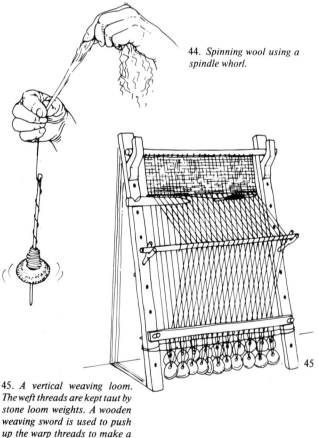

44. *Spinning wool using a spindle whorl.*

45. *A vertical weaving loom. The weft threads are kept taut by stone loom weights. A wooden weaving sword is used to push up the warp threads to make a closely woven textile.*

45

46

an important part of the community. Not all of the town's raw materials could be found locally and items such as iron, glass, building materials and precious metals were imported to provide work for other local craftsmen, such as carpenters, wrights and coopers, blacksmiths, armourers, glaziers, masons and other building workers. In addition to these, any town needed its service industries – millers, bakers, butchers, fishmongers and grocers. By the 14th century, many of the trades had formed themselves into guilds or incorporations. The crafts were grouped together under seven main headings – hammermen (including all metalworkers), bakers, wrights and coopers, tailors, shoemakers, weavers and fleshers (including all butchers and fishmongers). These Incorporated Trades are still in existence in the city today.

47

As in most medieval towns, tradesmen working in the same industries often tended to congregate in the same area. Sometimes this was for the convenience of being near to raw materials. Some crafts needed to be near to water; for example, workers in dyeing and fulling would need it for scouring their cloth, tanners needed water for soaking hides, while brewers also needed a source of fresh water. Potters not only required water, but also a convenient source of clay; because of the fire risk which went with their industry, they tended to be sited away from the centre of population. Similar anti-social industries were smithing, which caused constant noise and smell, and tanning, which involved soaking hides in vats of urine, which gave off noxious fumes. An example of such zoning of industries may be found on the west side of Gallowgate in the 14th century. A large quantity of leather off-cuts found on one site suggested the presence of a cobbler's workshop, whilst animal hair found on the same site may indicate the presence

46. *Wooden weaving sword. St Paul Street, 13th-14th century.*

47. *Clay pin mould. The heads and upper parts of two, possibly three pins, can be seen. At the top there is a decorated, rectangular head and in the centre, a plain circular one. Broad Street, 13th-14th century.*

48. *Fragments of the St Lawrence Bell or 'Old Lowrie'. This 17th-century bell is a recasting of the original, presented to the Church of St Nicholas in 1351 by William Leyth, Provost of Aberdeen.*

48

nearby of a tannery sited on the edge of the Loch. The bases of several kilns or ovens on an adjacent site are probably connected with this industry. This may tie in with the possibility of an early medieval flesh market with its associated butchery trade around Broad Street. Additional support for such specialised areas within the town may be found in street names such as Smithy Row (off the Gallowgate) in about 1400, and at a much later date, Tannery Street in the same area.

Most of our knowledge of these industries is based on historical records. The remains recovered from excavations have so far been fairly restricted. For example, despite the fact that the town clearly had a number of industries dependent upon textiles, we have found no remains of textile workshops or dyeworks. The main product which was being processed was wool. The raw fleeces were turned into finished cloth by a number of different processes. Spinning is represented by several spindle whorls of stone, antler and ivory (fig 44). After spinning, the yarn was woven into cloth on a vertical loom; our evidence for this is a wooden weaving sword and a loom weight (figs 45, 46). At any stage during these processes, the wool could be dyed, by soaking in a solution of plant and vegetable dyes. We can identify two of the basic dyes which were locally used. Some seeds of weld, which produced a bright yellow dye, were found in a cesspit at Queen Street, whilst a 14th-century document refers to an area in the Green known as the 'madderyard'; madder was universally used to produce reddish-brown cloth. We now have a considerable number of fragments of cloths and textiles from various sites in the city. Some of the finer cloths were probably imported from the Low Countries and England, but the coarser materials may have been made locally. So far, our evidence for the local industries suggests a fairly primitive technology, for example a weaving sword implies the use of a vertical loom, which is less efficient than the horizontal loom widely used in medieval Europe by the 13th century.

Another textile which may have been produced locally was linen. During the post-medieval period one of Aberdeen's major industries was flax-spinning and the presence of a large number of flax seeds in a cesspit at Queen Street suggests that this industry may already have evolved at an early date.

Geological examination of pottery fragments shows that, certainly from the 13th century onwards, pottery has been made in Aberdeen. The main output of the industry in its early days consisted of cooking-pots and jugs, but other vessel forms were also produced. The same kilns were probably used for firing pottery roof-tiles for use on buildings. As yet no traces of any medieval kilns have been found in the area, but two major sources of clay are known to exist, and were certainly exploited in the 18th and 19th centuries. The first of these was at Clayhills, which lay to the south-west of the medieval town, in the vicinity of modern Millburn

50

49. *A 16th-century illustration showing some of the stages in the production of coins by hand. Slices of bullion are flattened into blanks, weighed and trimmed to size, and hammered between two dies; the figure to right is seen holding the upper die in his left hand as he strikes the coin.*

50. *Silver groat, minted in Aberdeen during the reign of David II (1357-67). A groat was equivalent to four pennies.*

26

51. *A reconstruction of the interior of one of the late 13th or early 14th-century buildings excavated on St Paul Street. A woman is spinning wool by an open fire in the centre of the room; behind her, sits a man carding wool from a wicker basket at his feet. A loom stands at the end of the room. Space is at a premium, so things are hung from the roof, and stacked beneath the tables. To one side of the fire a chicken slowly roasts on a spit.*

Street. The name Clayhills was certainly in use by the end of the 14th century, and suggests that pottery must have been made there earlier than that date. A second source lay in Old Aberdeen, and was later exploited by the Seaton Potteries. It seems likely that either or both of these sources supplied the bulk of the pottery used in Aberdeen throughout the Middle Ages; although finer quality wares were imported, these always formed a minor element of the pottery assemblages.

The later 15th-century burgh records contain complaints about the noise made by smiths working in an area off the Gallowgate, possibly in or near Smithy Row. The term 'smith' probably includes coppersmiths, goldsmiths and silversmiths as well as blacksmiths. As yet we have found no evidence for iron smithing, but we have found a few moulds relating to the manufacture of objects in copper alloys such as bronze and brass. Many of the cauldrons and vessels used in kitchens were of copper alloy, but as they were commonly melted down for re-use when broken, they are not often found on excavations. However we have found the moulds for

two of them on a site in Gallowgate. Among other everyday items manufactured in thousands were pins and other dress fasteners. Part of a mould for some of these was found in Broad Street (fig 47). Apart from these commonplace items, the coppersmiths also produced more specialist products such as church bells and memorial brasses. Although we have yet to locate any of these industries, it is possible that the famous bells of St Nicholas' Church, known as St Lawrence and St Mary, were originally cast locally in the 14th century (fig 48).

A highly specialised form of metalworking is represented by moneyers. In the Middle Ages, all coinage manufacture was under royal control, but mints were operating in all the major cities at some point during the medieval period. The coins were produced by striking blanks between two dies (fig 49). Silver pennies struck in Aberdeen have been found in several Scottish coin hoards. We have no real idea where the Aberdeen mint was sited, nor do we know exactly when it was founded. There is a tradition that it was established by William

52. *Spit-roasting. Roasts would have been cooked in front of an open fire, the juices and fat being caught in a dripping pan positioned under the meat. From the 14th-century Luttrell Psalter.*

53. *A medieval feast. Laid on the trestle table is a varied selection of plates and bowls which could have been made from wood, leather and, in wealthy households, pewter, silver and gold. Knives and spoons are in evidence but the people at this 14th-century meal are using their hands to eat with. From manuscripts such as the Luttrell Psalter, from which this detailed illustration is taken, we can learn a lot about the appearance of the people of the time.*

the Lion, but coin evidence appears to suggest an even earlier date, perhaps during the final years of the reign of David I (1124-53).

The medieval burgh was surrounded by extensive tracts of land, some of which formed pasture and some of which were cultivated as town fields. The produce of these fields included quantities of grain which were ground at the town mills. Fortunately the two burghs were served by a number of fast-running burns and creeks, on which these mills were sited. To north-west of Old Aberdeen lay Gordon's Mills, certainly in existence by the 17th century and possibly much earlier, whilst New Aberdeen had a number of mills by the end of the Middle Ages. Within the area of the burgh itself, were the Flour Mill, between Upper and Nether Kirkgate, and the Trinity Mill, near the Trinitarian Friary, while a number were situated a little outside, for example the Justice Mills and the Gilcomston Mill. A mill does not exclusively imply the grinding of corn. Water was an important source of power for a number of processes, notably the fulling of cloth.

Eating and drinking

Throughout much of this period, most sections of burgh society would have done their cooking over an open fire in the centre of a building or room. This meant that methods were restricted to boiling, baking and spit-roasting (fig 52). During the 15th century this range was extended by the introduction of the frying-pan or skillet from the Low Countries. Most of the cooking was probably carried out in pottery and metal vessels, but a number of recipes also required boiling in skins. A modern survival of this practice is the haggis. Baking could be carried out either in the embers of the fire, or in special clay-built ovens. Small examples of these can be found inside buildings, but larger ones usually occur outside, e.g. at St Paul Street. The medieval diet was far more susceptible to fluctuations of weather and seasons than it is today. For long stretches of the winter, meat would either have been totally unavailable, or could be eaten only in a heavily salted and spiced form to disguise its rank flavour. Similarly, the availability of fish would be entirely dependent on catches. The range of vegetables that could be eaten was far more limited than it is today – only various forms of beans, green vegetables such as cabbage and kale, mushrooms and other fungi. This could be supplemented by dairy products such as eggs, butter and cheese, staples such as wheat, oats and barley, and whatever fruit and nuts were in season. Another source of fresh food were the shellfish which could be gathered in the estuaries of the Dee and the Don, while at least one of the friaries maintained a dovecot to provide additional meat and eggs. A certain amount of exotic spices and fruits might be available from time to time, but these would always have been expensive luxury items and in short supply. In the archaeological record, food remains are represented most commonly by animal and fish bones, but

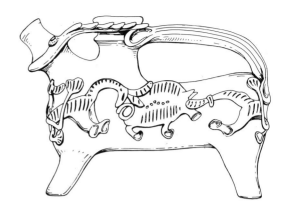

54

54. *An aquamanile – a pottery or metal jug, in the shape of an animal, used to carry water for washing the hands between courses. It was filled through a large spout in the animal's back; the water would then be poured through a smaller spout in the animal's head (either through its mouth or in the middle of its forehead) on to the person's hands, to be caught in a bowl.*

55

55. *A selection of some of the medieval pottery vessels which have been found in Aberdeen: 1. Low Countries grey-ware pitcher 2. Local jug 3. Cooking-pot from southern Scotland 4. Scarborough ware face-mask jug (from Yorkshire) 5. Rouen ware jug (from northern France) 6. Siegburg stoneware jug (from the Rhineland) 7 and 9. Local cooking-pots and jars 8. Urinal (a medieval chamber-pot) 10. Raeren stoneware drinking-mug (from the Rhineland) 11. A 'pirlie pig' or money-box 12. Paffrath ware ladle (from the Rhineland) 13. Valencian lustreware dish (from eastern Spain) 14. Skillet or frying-pan (from the Low Countries).*

occasionally in the form of seeds and other plant fragments preserved in cesspits. On all the sites so far excavated, the commonest bone remains are those of cattle, suggesting that beef was the most common type of meat eaten. The other bones included sheep, goat, pig, deer, fish, chickens, geese and the occasional wild bird. The excavation of 14th and 15th-century cesspits in the town have yielded the remains of raspberries, blaeberries, brambles, figs and grapes and various cereals such as wheat, barley and oats. Other plants present such as fat hen are now regarded as weeds, but were used as an additional spinach-like vegetable in times of shortage. The soil conditions on some of the Aberdeen sites are not always suitable for preserving the remains of edible shellfish, but examples of oysters, limpets, mussels, cockles, winkles and razor-shells have been found.

Water was widely available throughout the city from wells and burns, but this would have been little used for drinking as it must have been heavily polluted by the residues of the town's industries. The main types of drink would have been wine and ale. The first was imported in large quantities from south-west France and the Low Countries. Ale was brewed locally from barley, yeast and water; the addition of hops to produce beer was not introduced into Britain until the very late Middle Ages. Ale could be drunk either in a strong form called porter, or as a watered-down version which later became known as small beer. Some sort of grain spirit was presumably also available.

Most of the dishes, bowls, plates and tankards in use on the table would have been made of wood or leather, although vessels in pewter, silver and gold would have been in use in houses of higher status (fig 53). In most households, drink would have been served in pottery jugs, some of which were imported from some distance away (south-west France, Holland or Belgium). The commonest utensil was the table knife (usually with a bone or wooden handle), which also served the function of the modern fork. Spoons of wood, pewter and silver would have been in use, but much eating was done with the hands. To cope with this, large pottery or metal vessels, called aquamaniles (fig 54), often in the form of exotic animals, were filled with water to wash the hands between courses in a bowl called a laver. The archae-ological evidence for all these vessels and utensils is often fragmentary, because many of the organic materials such as wood, leather and bone, have not survived. At St Paul Street, a couple of birchwood bowls (fig 56) and a wooden spoon have survived by chance, but by far the most common finds are the pottery jugs (fig 55).

Clothing, personal possessions and leisure

Excavations within the town have produced numerous fragments of cloth, leather and dress-fastenings. The finest piece of cloth was part of a woollen gown and had probably been imported from England or the Low Countries (fig 57), but the majority, although probably

56

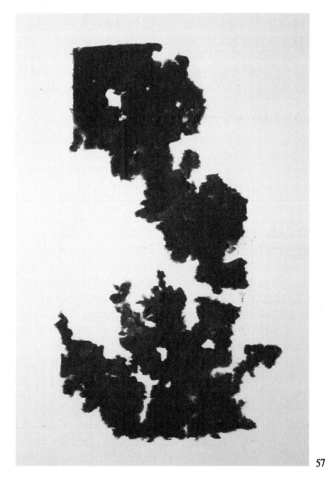

57

56. *Birch-wood bowls. St Paul Street, 14th century.*

57. *Fragment of fine wool cloth, imported from the Low Countries. Queen Street, 13th-14th century.*

58A

58. *A. 14th-century footwear, including a child's shoe-sole.*
    B. Medieval shoes were of a 'turnshoe' construction, that is the sole was stitched to the upper and then the shoe was turned inside out.

58B

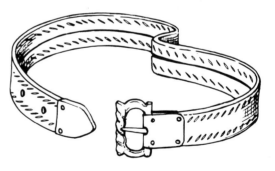

59B

59. *A. Part of a decorated leather belt. Queen Street, 13th-14th century.*
    B. The belt in use with a buckle found in Virginia Street.

59A

31

clothing fragments, are obviously of a much poorer quality. Woollen garments included gowns, plaids, shawls, tunics and hose, but in most cases it is difficult to say much about the original form of the garment, because so much of the cloth has obviously been re-used as rags before being disposed of.

Leather would have been used much more widely than it is today. The commonest remains are the soles and uppers of boots and shoes (fig 58). Clearly these were a valuable commodity. Most of those found have been worn into holes and patched again and again. Only a shoe-sole suitable for a child of about two has come to us virtually unworn, presumably because a child of that age would not have had the chance to wear out his shoes in the same way as an adult. Footwear is a particularly intimate and poignant find, because the pattern of wear on the soles and uppers hints at the shape of the owner's feet, complete with deformities, corns and bunions. Leather was also used for fastenings; besides belts, leather thongs or laces were used to fasten jerkins. Lastly, hides and skins were one of the best sources of weatherproof clothing.

Clothes could also be fastened with brooches, buckles, pins, buttons and toggles (fig 60). Sometimes bone or copper buttons were covered in a textile to match the garment to which they were sewn. One delicate buckle was fashioned in the form of bird-heads (fig 62), while the shape of penannular brooches is still very familiar to us today.

Some of the many pins found may have been used in hairdressing, while a fragment of Italian silk ribbon with delicate picoted edging must have adorned the hair of a fashionable 14th-century lady (fig 63). Another evocative reminder of the care some people took of their appearance is given by a small antler comb (fig 64).

Evidence for leisure pursuits is understandably scanty, but occasional finds offer a glimpse of how people spent their free time, for example a bone skate (fig 65), or various gaming counters and dice.

Just how healthy were they?

For many people in medieval Aberdeen, life must have been short, brutal and painful. It is difficult for many of us to imagine an existence totally without flushing toilets, properly insulated houses, adequate heating and lighting, clean water supply and medical advice. In some ways it seems surprising that they survived at all. Since 1981, a research project at the Department of Anatomy, Marischal College, has examined the human skeletons found during excavations at the Carmelite Friary site to give us precise details of the health and stature of Aberdonians from the 14th to 17th centuries, and an indication of how they did manage to contend with their difficult lifestyle (fig 67).

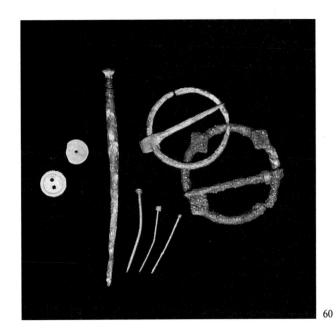

60

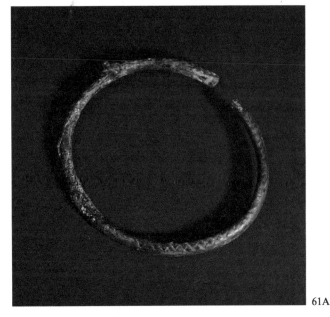

61A

61B

60. *A selection of clothes fasteners found on various sites in Aberdeen. 13th-14th century.*

61. *A. Decorated copper alloy bracelet.*
    B. As it was found, around the left wrist of a male skeleton at the Carmelite Friary.

62. *Copper alloy buckle decorated with twin bird heads. Broad Street, 13th-14th century.*

63. *Fragment of silk ribbon. Broad Street, 14th century.*

64. *Antler comb. St Paul Street, 14th century.*

62

63

64

65A

65. *Bone ice skate made from the metatarsal of a horse (A). The medieval skater would have stood on his skates and propelled himself along the ice with the help of a pole (B). Although some medieval bone skates do have holes to allow the skater to attach them to his feet, this example does not. It was unnecessary as the skates were never lifted from the surface of the ice. Queen Street, 13th-14th century.*

65B

66. *Oak coracle paddle (A). A coracle is a small craft, circular or oblong in shape, made from animal hides stretched over a wicker frame (B). The hook at the end of the paddle handle would have been used to lift the coracle on to the back for carrying. St Paul Street, 13th-14th century.*

66B

66A

67

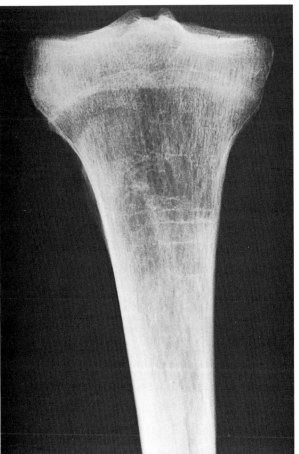

68

Of the 126 or so skeletons excavated, over half were adult, but the remainder were under 25 years of age. This is not unexpected, since young children would be highly susceptible to diseases such as measles and influenza, which most of us shrug off today, particularly if they lived in unhygienic conditions and suffered from malnutrition.

A study of their skeletons allows us to record some of the diseases and injuries which troubled Aberdonians in the medieval period, although of course we only see those ailments which have affected the bones. Only very rarely is it possible to ascertain from the skeleton a cause of death, except in the case of obviously serious injury, or where an illness has been so long-term that it has begun to affect the bones, as might be the case with chronic diseases such as leukaemia, or secondary tumours from a soft-tissue cancer. Many diseases, among them cholera, plague and smallpox, which kill quickly and only affect the body tissue, cannot be detected. It must also be remembered, that in the days before antibiotics, a simple chest infection could be fatal or an infected wound cause death from septicaemia within a few days. So, for example, we have a man in apparently full health apart from a healed sprained ankle, who died in his mid-30s, from an unknown cause.

The limb bones and teeth of skeletons can give an indication of the health of an individual during his formative years. If children do become seriously ill, they stop growing until they recover. Such periods of arrested growth may be detected on the teeth and bones (fig 68). One repercussion of periods of illness during growth may be the shorter stature of medieval Aberdonians, compared with their modern counterparts: medieval men tended to an average height of 5ft 5in compared with 5ft 10in today, while women averaged 5ft 2in compared with a modern 5ft 5in. It is noticeable that there is less difference in height between medieval and modern women than between medieval and modern men; female children have always tended not to be so susceptible to illness as males and on the whole therefore to develop better.

Examination of the skeletons can also reveal which injuries and diseases afflicted medieval Aberdonians. Apart from traumatic injuries such as fractures, other problems identified have included tuberculosis, spina bifida and arthritis. Some fractures have healed remarkably well. One individual had ribs fractured and healed in at least two places along the length of the rib, a badly sprained ankle and a sprained wrist. One adult male suffered a depressed fracture of the skull as the result of a blow with a blunt instrument. The hole in the skull is very apparent, but its edges are smooth and round, showing that the damage healed without infection. In life the hole would have been covered with

67. *Some of the burials excavated at the Carmelite Friary.*

68. *X-ray of an adult tibia (shin bone) taken at knee level. The fine white lines passing horizontally across the shaft are commonly known as Harris lines. They represent episodes of arrested growth due to periods of illness or malnutrition during childhood.*

a tough fibrous tissue, in order to protect the delicate brain (fig 69).

It is clear that arthritis affected the hands and spines of earlier Aberdonians as much as it affects their descendents today (fig 70). Arthritic changes lead to diminished mobility in joints and severe pain, as loss of cartilage covering the joint causes bone to rub against bone, producing a polished surface. Interestingly there is no evidence of the arthritic hip, a common ailment today in older individuals, probably because in the medieval period people simply did not live sufficiently long. One person suffered from arthritic thumbs and fingers, particularly on her left hand, suggesting her lifestyle included constant use of her hands and that she may have been left-handed. Many older Aberdonians endured degenerative changes in the vertebral column as a result of age-related lipping around the margins of the vertebrae; sometimes this became so extensive that two adjacent vertebrae fused together. This would have given rise to the kind of pain in the lower back from which many people suffer even today without any obvious clinical cause.

Close scrutiny of the teeth of these people has given an indication of their oral health and hygiene as well as the nature of their diet. Some of their dental problems are all too familiar to us today. Gingivitis, or gum disease, was rampant, leading to gum recession and eventual loss of teeth. But in some ways the pattern of tooth decay was different from ours. It is clear that their diet was rough and fibrous compared with our modern refined foods. Such a diet, particularly small pieces of grit in their flour, caused the white enamel to wear down, exposing the yellowish dentine, which makes up the bulk of the teeth. An advantage of such wear is a reduced tendency to decay on the chewing surfaces of the teeth, as compared with those of modern people. Instead medieval teeth tended to develop areas of decay on the sides as a result of damage to the enamel or the build-up of large deposits of calculus through poor oral hygiene. Where tooth surfaces were severely worn, root abscesses developed. In cases where the tooth was not extracted or the abscess drained the pressure of the accumulated pus gradually wore through the bone giving rise to open and extremely painful cavities around the root. The owner of such a tooth must surely have been greatly relieved when it eventually loosened and fell out altogether (fig 72).

In addition to the evidence of skeletal remains, environmental samples taken during excavations have provided a little background to the health of medieval people in Aberdeen. In a period where modern sanitation was unknown, much human waste found its way into cesspits, whose residues can be a valuable source of information to the archaeologist. In one such pit at St Paul Street were numerous eggs of a roundworm parasite known to infect human intestines (fig 73). Such parasites seem, from evidence from excavations elsewhere, to have been almost endemic among medieval populations. Parasitic infestation

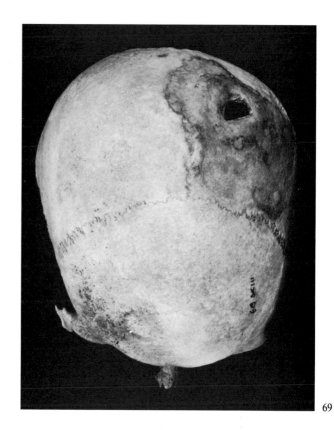

69

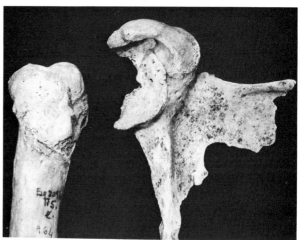

70

69. *Adult male with a healed depressed fracture of the skull. The large hole in the top left-hand side of the skull represents a depressed fracture. Such an injury may have been caused by a blow to the head with a blunt instrument, or by falling against a rounded object.*

70. *Adult shoulder showing severe osteo-arthritic changes. These bones show destruction of the shoulder joint, with the loss of the humeral head and gross lipping around the margins of the joint. The polished bones would have been extremely painful. The arm would have been shortened and the joint would have been stiff and inflamed.*

36

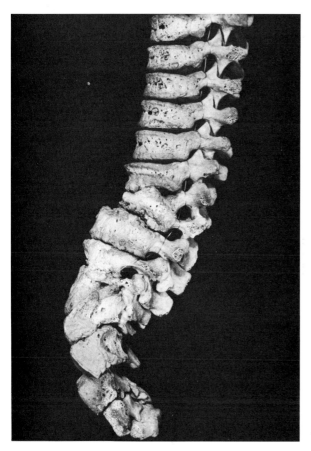

71

significantly lowers the resistance to illness, and particularly in conjunction with poor standards of hygiene and nutrition may have been an important factor in the susceptibility of medieval Aberdonians to illness. Seeds of some plants also found in rubbish and cesspits may suggest their use as purgatives to combat such conditions – for example it is possible that figs were imported for that very purpose. In another pit at St Paul Street, the tracing of seeds of the opium poppy may indicate its use as a sedative, perhaps to alleviate some of the aches and pains which must otherwise have been excruciating.

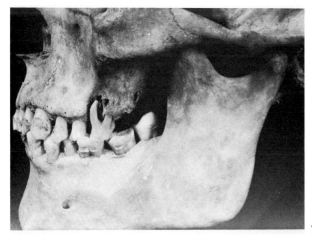

72

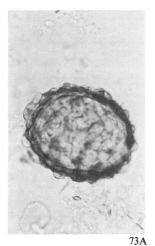

73A

73B

71. *Lower vertebral column of 8-10 year old child showing the effects of healed tuberculosis. There is marked destruction in the lower spine, as shown by the rough, pitted surfaces and irregular shape of the bodies of the vertebrae. The resulting collapse of the vertebrae may have resulted in the child being paralysed from the waist down due to damage to the spinal nerves.*

72. *Adult skull showing evidence of a long-standing abscess in the jaw, around the roots of the upper left first molar. Erosion of the bony socket, caused by the pressure of the accumulated pus, has resulted in the exposure of the roots. If this individual had lived longer, the tooth would have become so loose that it would have eventually fallen out. The teeth show severe, uneven wear of the chewing surface as a result of a rough, fibrous diet. There is also evidence of calculus deposits on the surface of the teeth.*

73. *The highly magnified eggs of parasitic worms Ascaris (A) and Trichuris (B), found in a cesspit during the Queen Street excavations. Both these worms are common parasites of man and his domestic animals, especially pigs.*

4. Life in the post-medieval town

In the period between 1500 and 1800, the burgh of New Aberdeen was to be greatly transformed, as it grew both in wealth and importance (fig 74). Its buildings were to change dramatically both in size and in appearance – with the introduction of new building materials and an ever-increasing demand for more housing. Nor was this change confined simply to houses and flats: the character of its churches and chapels was to change markedly – particularly after the disappearance of its monasteries, following the Reformation. The rapidly growing burgh also needed more public buildings – colleges, grammar school, Customs House and Weigh House were all to be built during this period – and those which were already in existence were to be rebuilt on a grander scale (e.g. the Tolbooth and the Mercat Cross). Population growth was to lead to overcrowding, which in turn brought its own problems – the risk of fire and disease breaking out in the more densely inhabited quarters was ever present: thus, this period sees a growing consciousness of the need for public welfare and public health measures – fire regulations and the purchase of a fire engine, the introduction of a piped water supply (of sorts) and a host of regulations about the disposal of rubbish and the cleaning-up of the city's wells and other water sources.

In Old Aberdeen, King's College grew to fill the vacuum provided by the decline of St Machar's Cathedral after the Reformation (fig 75). The availability of extensive tracts of open land meant that the burgh was able to expand from the High Street to the south along the road to New Aberdeen, and never suffered from the same problems of overcrowding which affected its more prosperous neighbour.

Changes were also taking place in everyday households. Not only were rooms becoming smaller, warmer, better lit and cosier than their draughty medieval fore-runners, but fashions were changing in dress, in furniture and in household articles; even methods of cooking were to change, with the proliferation of completely new vessels, such as the frying-pan and the chafing-dish (a sort of 'casserole night-light') (fig 77). Cheap stoneware drinking-mugs were to replace the older wooden and leather tankards; similarly, pottery plates and dishes were to replace latten and pewter vessels on most people's tables. The importation of large numbers of glass vessels was to bring wine bottles and drinking-glasses into almost every household. Yet this was just the tip of the iceberg: the far-flung trading connections of the port were to bring goods of every description from all over north-west Europe, the Mediterranean and the colonies into everyday circulation, and were even to introduce new social habits, such as the taking of snuff and the smoking of tobacco, or later on, the drinking of tea and of coffee.

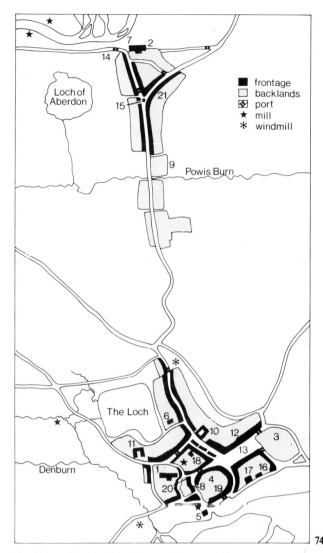

74. *Old and New Aberdeen from the 16th to the 18th century, with the main buildings mentioned in the text. THE CHURCHES: 1. St Nicholas' 2. St Machar's 3. St Ninian's Chapel 4. St Katherine's Chapel 5. Trinity Church 6. St Paul's, Gallowgate THE HOSPITALS: 7. St Mary's Hospital 8. St Thomas's Hospital THE COLLEGES: 9. King's College 10. Marischal College 11. The Grammar School PUBLIC BUILDINGS AND INSTITUTIONS: 12. The Tolbooth 13. Flesh and Fish Markets, and Mercat Cross 14. Old Market Stance in Old Aberdeen 15. The Townhouse, Old Aberdeen 16. Customs House 17. Weigh House NOTABLE SURVIVING STANDING BUILDINGS: 18. Provost Skene's House 19. Provost Ross's House 20. Original position of the 'Wallace Tower' 21. The Bede House.*

75. *King's College, Old Aberdeen, with its famous crown steeple, was founded by Bishop William Elphinstone in 1495.*

76. *Portrait of John Alexander and his wife, Marjory Jamesone. Attributed to Aberdeen artist George Jamesone (1588-1644).*

75

76

Most of these changes lie outside the scope of this work: in fact, to do them justice, would warrant a book in its own right. Moreover, as most of our excavations have so far been concentrated on medieval sites within the town, we can as yet contribute very little from an archaeological viewpoint to our understanding of this period; however, we can at least say a little about the kind of buildings in which people lived and worshipped.

Later houses and shops

Between the years 1400 and 1700, the population of the burgh was to almost double (to about 6,000), and in the following century was to redouble (to a little over 12,000). Hence, the pressure on housing space, which was already building up in the later Middle Ages, was to persist and intensify; and the same measures, which were adopted then to deal with the problem, continued to be applied throughout this period: more houses were built at right-angles to the street frontage (fig 78): the buildings on the frontages became increasingly higher, and were split into numerous flats, approached by external staircases, which jutted out into the street: and more and more buildings were constructed in the backlands. In 1661 Parson Gordon described the town as follows:

'The houses are built of stone and lime, and have sloping roofs covered with slates. Most of them are three-storied, and not a few rise to a height of four flats. The streets are laid with flint or a very hard stone resembling flint. The dwellings are very beautiful outside and inside, and where (for they usually show gardens or orchards adjoining them, and have their own back gates for particular gardens) they look out on the street, they are adorned with wooden porches. They are also planted round with trees of all kinds suitable to the district, so that the whole town presents the appearance of a grove to those approaching it.'

The map which accompanies his description would seem to confirm this picture of large areas of gardens and orchards within the town, although almost every close is shown as having some buildings or outhouses within it. However, by the time that we get to Milne's map of 1789 (fig 79), the appearance of the town has changed dramatically: whilst the shape of the medieval rigs is still preserved in the stone boundary walls of the plots, most of the gardens and orchards have long since disappeared beneath buildings, and many of the built-up courts and pends which came to typify the 19th-century town centre, are already in existence.

The extract which we have quoted above, comes from a very long and detailed description of both New and Old Aberdeen by Parson Gordon. You might well ask, if we have such good early maps of the town, and such detailed contemporary descriptions of it, do we really need to search any further to find out what the town looked like? The simple answer is yes, because although these are valuable sources of information about the shape and nature of Aberdeen during this period, they should not be taken too literally. Neither Gordon's nor

77

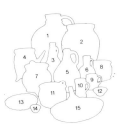

77. A selection of some of the post-medieval pottery vessels which have been found in Aberdeen: 1. A local jug or pitcher 2. Large local storage jar 3. Frechen stoneware Bellarmine (a type of jug made in the Rhineland: they were so called after the bearded faces on their necks, which were said to be modelled on a Cardinal Bellarmine) 4. A local pipkin (handled cooking-pot) 5. Raeren stoneware jug (from the Rhineland) 6. Frechen stoneware drinking-mug (from the Rhineland) 7. Dutch pipkin 8. Northern Dutch tin-glazed drug-jar (so-called 'delftware', after the town of Delft) 9. English tin-glazed tankard 10. Local iron-glazed tyg (a type of mug or tankard with two or more handles) 11. Westerwald stoneware chamber-pot (from the Rhineland) 12. Small tin-glazed bowl, either English or Dutch 13. Staffordshire white salt-glazed stoneware plate 14. Chinese porcelain tea-bowl 15. Local dripping-pan.

78

78. Building in the High Street, Old Aberdeen, with its gable facing on to the road.

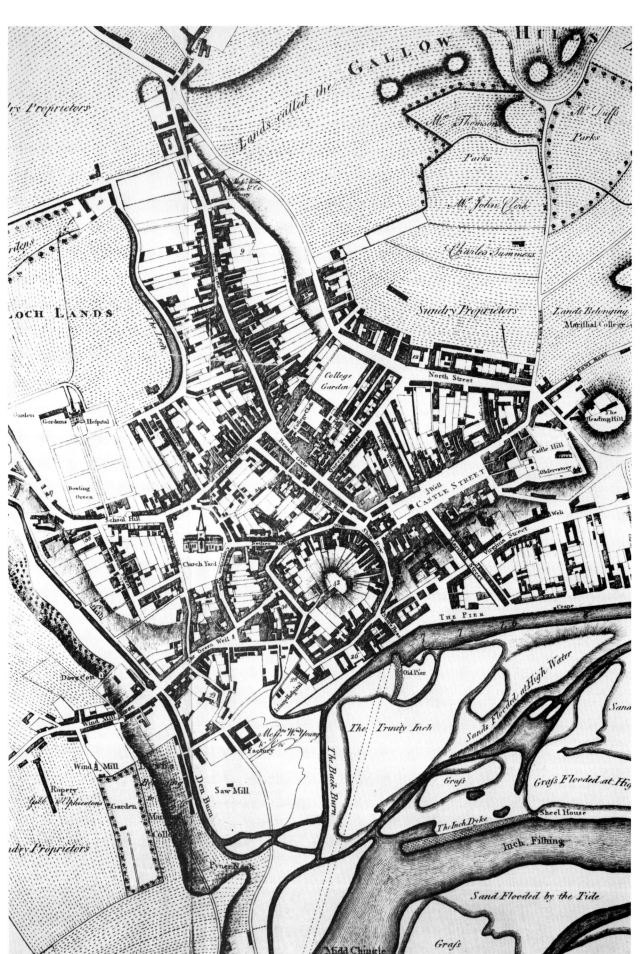

79. *A detail from Milne's map of 1789.*

Milne's map was ever meant to be an accurate street by street, house by house record, in the way that a modern Ordnance Survey map is – Gordon's map, in particular, is heavily stylised, and it is really impossible to state with any certainty what structures may have stood on any one plot. Similarly, although his description gives us a very vivid picture of Aberdeen in the middle years of the 17th century, it is certainly not a complete one, and a mass of evidence is now accumulating, both from excavations, and from delving in contemporary documents, to suggest that his account is misleading, notably about the materials used in building construction, and also about the form of the houses themselves. First, his account makes no mention of a very strong tradition of building in timber in the town; at the beginning of this period, the majority of buildings in both burghs were still being built in timber, and 'wooden' (or timber-framed) houses were to continue to be erected throughout this period – despite a ban on their construction in 1741; in fact, some of the last examples were still standing in the Gallowgate as late as 1840.

Secondly, the use of slates as a roofing material had not replaced thatching anywhere near as completely as his account would suggest. Even as Gordon was writing his text, large public buildings such as the Grammar School were still thatched, and the use of this material continued to be widespread throughout the period – despite ineffectual bans in 1716 and 1741; in the 1780s only four of the cottages in the fishing village of Footdee had slate roofs all the rest were thatched; and in 1826, a fire in King Street started in the heather-thatched roof of a cottage, which must have been built after 1802.

Thirdly, whilst three and four-storeyed buildings certainly did exist on some of the main frontages, they were by no means the only type of buildings which proliferated there; whilst Gordon's map presents us with a fairly uniform picture of the principal frontages, the reality was probably much more of a hotch-potch, with buildings of all shapes and sizes – some in stone, some timber-framed – whilst in the backlands, there may also have been clay-walled and post-and-wattle buildings.

All of the surviving historic buildings in the city were built of stone. Some of the earlier ones are of sandstone, but as this material is not found locally, it had to be brought from quite a distance; because of the extra cost involved, its use was largely restricted to prestige buildings (e.g. King's College), or to small intricately carved details, such as stones with inscribed dates or coats-of-arms. The stone which was most commonly used in both burghs was granite; although nowhere near as easy to carve, it was cheap and readily available. Most house walls were built of rubble and boulders, bonded together with clay or with lime mortar; the only shaping or dressing involved was on the stones at the corners of buildings, and around the edges of doors and windows. By the beginning of the 18th century, another building material came into use: brick. Although very

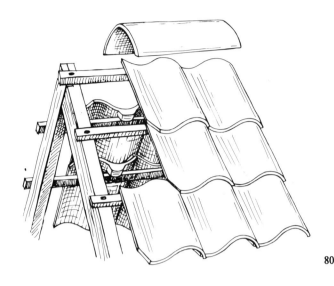

80

81

80. *A pantiled roof. A small projecting stub or collar on the back of the tile hangs directly on to the rafter, and each S-shaped tile is carefully overlapped. The ridge of the roof is capped with a plain long ridge tile which is semi-circular in section.*

81. *The 'Wallace Tower' was originally built in about 1600 in the Nether Kirkgate. In 1964 it was dismantled to make way for the present Marks and Spencers store, and was re-erected in Seaton Park.*

82

83

84

82. *Provost Ross's House in the Shiprow. Originally built in 1593, it has been substantially altered during the 18th century. Together with the two adjoining 18th-century houses, it now houses Aberdeen's Maritime Museum.*

83. *Mar's Castle was built in 1595, and stood at the top of the Gallowgate. It bore many similarities to its contemporary, Provost Ross's House. It was pulled down for road widening in 1896.*

84. *Provost Skene's House in the Guestrow. The oldest part of the building dates from 1545, but most of the present structure belongs to the 1626 and 1669 rebuildings. It is now a period museum.*

few buildings were built entirely of this new material, it was widely used for details such as hearths and chimney-stacks, and for lining the surrounds of doors and windows. Another material which was manufactured in the same local kilns as these bricks, was the pantile; these became very popular, and seem to have been used almost as widely as slates – many can still be seen on buildings in Old Aberdeen today (fig 80). Where buildings of this date have been excavated in the city, they have had either cobbled, or beaten earth floors; plank floors do not seem to have been introduced until the early 19th century. Quite often, there was a step down into the buildings: the continual repairing of the streets and pends outside resulted in these surfaces being at a different level to the adjacent buildings. The open hearths of the medieval houses were increasingly replaced by proper fireplaces (first, in stone, and later, in brick), set against the walls; initially, many had daub-lined smoke-hoods, but these were later phased out in favour of stone and brick chimneys. All of the excavated buildings had glass windows by the middle of the 17th century; the glass was cut into fairly small rectangular or lozenge-shaped panes, which were held in place by small strips of lead.

The buildings which still survive, or which stood until recently, are mostly the better built houses of the gentry and the wealthier sections of society; hence, they are not necessarily typical of the buildings in which most people lived. Those can now be studied only by exca-vation. Nevertheless, we can distinguish a number of different house types amongst these structures: tower-houses and large town-houses, three and four-storeyed tenements, smaller houses and cottages.

Tower-houses and town-houses

The best example of a tower-house in the city now stands in Tillydrone Park. This is the so-called 'Wallace Tower' (Keith of Benholm's lodging) which originally stood in the Nether Kirkgate (fig 81). It is a tall building with a Z-shaped plan, which was closely modelled on the castles which were then being built in the surrounding countryside; features, such as the small gun-loops under some of the ground-floor windows would hardly have been necessary in the Nether Kirkgate. It dates to about 1600, and is probably the most flamboyant of the large town-houses. A more modest example of this date can be seen in Provost Ross's House in the Shiprow (fig 82). Although much altered by later additions, this began life in 1593 as a simple, rectangular building at right-angles to the street, and with projecting towers at the front and back. A similar building of 1595 (Mar's Castle) used to stand at the top of the Gallowgate, before it was pulled down for road-widening at the turn of the century (fig 83). On both of these buildings, projecting rows of stones (corbels) running around the upper parts of the walls are modelled on contemporary castle architecture. The only other surviving town-house of the 16th century is Provost Skene's House in Guestrow (fig 84). This is one of the best-known landmarks in the city centre, but

85

86

85. *The Bede House, Don Street, Old Aberdeen. It was originally built in 1676 for Baillie William Logan and his wife Janet Moir. In 1786 it was acquired as a replacement for the old Bishop's Hospital, to house eight Bedemen – poor, unmarried men of 60 years or more; this use ended after a few years, and it has since been used as a private dwelling house.*

86. *64, Shiprow at the time of its demolition in 1876. Built in 1692, it was typical of a range of three-storeyed buildings with attics which once characterised the major streets in the town. Of the two doorways, the one on the left led to the upper floors, the one on the right to the ground floor shop. The first floor windows are still in their original form, but those on the second floor have been replaced at a later date.*

most of the present structure dates from the extensive modifications and rebuildings of 1626 and 1669. It originally started life in 1545 as a fairly modest and straightforward building with an L-shaped ground plan: this gave one wing running parallel to Guestrow, and another extending back at right-angles into the close. Although these are now the only surviving examples of the large town-houses of the gentry, they were by no means the most important houses in the town in their day; there is ample documentary evidence for many of the more important families building new stone houses in the Castlegate in the first half of the 16th century – but these have long since disappeared and we have no idea of just how typical any of the surviving structures are. One thing which we can say, is that some of their features, such as their crow-stepped gables and circular stair-towers, recur on many of the bigger buildings put up in the 17th and 18th centuries – very good examples of these can be seen on the Bede House in Old Aberdeen (fig 85).

Three and four-storeyed tenements

Tall tenement blocks were prominent features of many of the larger Scottish towns during this period. In Edinburgh and Glasgow, buildings of seven or more storeys were by no means unknown; however, there is no evidence to suggest that Aberdeen ever boasted anything on this scale. The largest blocks appear to have been in the Green and on Shiprow, and were served by external wooden forestairs; unfortunately, these were pulled down long before the advent of photography, and they are not recorded in any early engravings or sketches. There is certainly no modern tradition of building tall tenements in the city, and it seems reasonable to assume that old tenement blocks were unlikely to be replaced by anything smaller in the 18th and 19th centuries; hence, we are likely to be dealing with buildings of three or four storeys high (as Parson Gordon implied in the extract quoted above).

The only buildings of this size which survived until recently were the more modest dwellings belonging to the prominent burgesses. We have very little idea of how these compared to the tenement blocks in either size or shape; certainly, the fact that so many of these burgess houses survived until the latter years of the 19th century suggests that they were much better built, and probably far more comfortable to live in. A typical example of these buildings stood at 64 Shiprow, and was constructed in 1692 (fig 86). It was a three-storeyed house with an attic lit by dormer windows; at the time of its demolition, access to its upper floors was by an internal staircase, entered through a separate door from the street, and it seems quite likely that this was always the case. The surrounds of its door and windows were lined with dressed granite. In some cases these buildings were originally L-shaped in plan; in other cases they were extended into an L-shape, by the addition of an extra wing to their rear.

87A

87B

87. Marischal Street is the only surviving example of a Georgian thoroughfare in Aberdeen (A). Built between 1766 and 1773, it was the first street in the city to be paved with squared granite setts. Many of the houses still have fine examples of wrought iron-work (B).

88

89

46

90A

The later 18th-century equivalents of these houses can still be seen in Castle Street and Marischal Street. The latter is the only complete example of a Georgian street left in the city; it was laid out between 1766 and 1773, and was the first street to be paved with granite setts. Many of its elegant three-storeyed buildings have fine fanlit doorways, and there are several good examples of wrought-iron balustrades and shoescrapers (fig 87).

Smaller houses and cottages

As well as these larger buildings, two-storeyed houses with attics could occasionally be found on some of the frontages, and along the pends behind them; occasional 18th-century examples, such as 17 Castle Street, still survive, and it is likely that these replaced 17th-century buildings of similar size. Behind these frontages, low two-storeyed 'cottages' were split into a number of flats (fig 88); those on the first floor were entered by a separate staircase, which could either be inside or outside the building – a number of 18th-century cottages with external wooden staircases were still standing in the Hardweird in Gilcomston towards the end of the last century (fig 89).

Most of the buildings which we have been looking at so far have been in the centre of New Aberdeen, where building space was at a premium; but in places like Old Aberdeen and the fishing village of Footdee (both of which lie within the modern city boundaries, but which have a very distinct character and enjoyed a separate development), there was far less overcrowding, and in consequence, there are many more small houses and cottages. A row of single-storeyed cottages, dating from 1732, can still be seen in 1-3 Grant Place, Old Aberdeen; whilst an early 18th-century row of two-storeyed buildings stands nearby in 3-5 Wrights' and Coopers' Place (fig 90). Whilst all of these have now been restored, they are quite typical of the kind of buildings which could be found around the outskirts of Aberdeen in the 18th century – as is clear from the following description of Footdee in the 1780s:

'The town consisted of several rows of low thatched cottages, running from east to west, between the high road and the Harbour . . . Nothing could be more apparently comfortless than the exterior of those dwellings, each fronting the back of the opposite neighbour, and the narrow space between forming a line of dung hills crossed over with supporting spars from which hung lines, bladders and buoys, intermingled with dried skate and dog fish.'

88. *A reconstruction of Albion Court as it might have appeared in the late 17th century. This terrace of two-storeyed buildings was probably split into flats, which required separate entrances to the upper floor. In about 1760 the entire terrace was rebuilt at the same time as the Castlegate frontage (approached through the pend or alley-way on the left of the drawing).*

89. *George Washington Wilson's photograph of the Hardweird in Gilcomston. Some of these two-storeyed dwellings with their external stone staircases and pantiled roofs date from the later 18th century; the others are probably of 19th-century date.*

90. *Examples of smaller buildings in Old Aberdeen dating to the early 18th century. A single-storeyed terrace in Grant's Place built in 1732 (A). A two-storeyed terrace in Wrights' and Coopers' Place (B).*

90B

Later churches and chapels

In Scotland the Reformation was by no means a sudden event. In 1560, after some 20 years of increasing dissatisfaction with much within the Church and the degeneration of the monastic lifestyle, papal authority was formally abolished by Parliament. However it was not until 1688 that Presbyterianism triumphed, and for over 100 years after the 'official' date of the Reformation the alternation between episcopal and presbyterian ascendancy caused a period of great uncertainty. As a result, there was little church building in Aberdeen or elsewhere in the later 16th or 17th centuries and a pattern evolved of gradual change of the existing buildings to suit new forms of worship. For many Aberdeen churches the first 40 or so years after 1560 would have been a period of dereliction and decay, made worse by the fact that in the pre-Reformation years so much finance had been appropriated away from the local churches towards monasteries, cathedrals or secular interests.

In December 1559, a force recruited in Angus and the Mearns made its way north to 'reform' Aberdeen. The

91. *The monument at St Machar's Cathedral, to Bishop Patrick Scougal, who died in 1685. The architect was John Montgomery of Old Rayne, who also built Aberdeen's fine Mercat Cross in Castle Street.*

92. *St Nicholas' Church in the 19th century. The two churches, East and West, are clearly shown. The present East Church of St Nicholas was designed by the Aberdeen architect Archibald Simpson and built in 1837. The West Church, a fine example of an 18th-century church, was designed by James Gibbs, also a native of Aberdeen, and built between 1751 and 1755.*

91

92

48

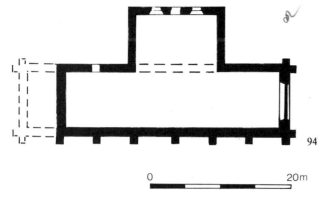

94

0   20m

94. *Plan of Greyfriars Church, showing the alterations carried out in the 18th century. The original church is shown in dotted line.*

friaries were subject to particular attack because they were especially accessible and the popularity of the friars as preachers may have been considered a threat to reformation. The Town Council Registers record that the reforming force had entered the places of the Black and White Friars, taken away their 'gere and guids', timber work, roof lead and slates to apply to their own particular uses. Looting rather than wholesale destruction was the object of the exercise, and the Council's concern lay mainly in ensuring that the goods removed became their property rather than that of the looters. The Town Council was in little sympathy with reforming tendencies, and took care that many of the treasures of St Nicholas' were placed in safe keeping before the arrival of the Reformers. However, at both St Nicholas' and St Machar's damage was undoubtedly done to windows and woodwork, hangings and paintings, although there is some evidence that both buildings were in some need of repair well before the Reformation.

At the Reformation the major problem was that existing church buildings, constructed to accommodate a large staff of clergy and numerous altars and services, were totally unfit for the new forms of worship centred around one minister whose main role was to preach. Churches tended therefore to be subdivided, or the unnecessary parts of them just left to deteriorate and collapse; as a result, by 1690, when Parliament abolished episcopacy in favour of presbyterianism, the appearance of Aberdeen churches had greatly changed from that of 150 years before. St Machar's became the parish church of Old Aberdeen after the Reformation, superseding the Snow Kirk, and by 1569 had a regular minister, although little seems to have been done to maintain or improve the fabric until 1607. By that time the cathedral had been more severely depleted when the roof lead was removed to pay for the Regent's troops. Around 1650 the walls of the choir were demolished so that the stone could be re-used in the fort on Castle Hill. But at a much earlier stage a wall had been built cutting off the choir from the nave and crossing and relieving the building of unnecessary length. St Machar's was finally reduced to very much its modern external appearance, after the tower collapsed in 1688 and a wall was built across the east of the nave. Inside the church, by 1690, the principal members of the congregation, lairds, scholars, merchants and craftsmen showed their status by increasingly elaborate 'desks' or lofts, while those of lower rank sat with the women and children in the body of the kirk. The Parish Church of St Nicholas was divided in two by stone walls in 1596, to form the East and West Churches with the north and south transepts forming a no-man's-land (fig 92).

93

93. *Interior of West Church of St Nicholas.*

Of the former friary churches, by 1690, the Carmelite and Dominican churches were disused, certainly ruined and possibly no longer visible, the Trinitarians' church still stood and may have been used intermittently, while Greyfriars had become the church of the College founded by the Earl Marischal on the friary site.

St Ninian's Chapel on Castle Hill, although occasionally used for religious purposes – it is said that Bishop Patrick Forbes lay in state in the chapel in 1635 – served various secular uses, as a lighthouse, a court-house, a gunpowder store and a prison for Quakers until it was demolished in 1794 when Castle Hill was leased to the Government. The chapel on St Katherine's Hill probably went out of use at the Reformation. Of the hospitals, only St Mary's in Old Aberdeen and St Thomas's continued after the Reformation. The former was certainly in existence into the 18th century.

The next major development in Aberdeen churches took place in the 18th century. By now the Church was on a steadier financial footing, and required to consolidate its position by erecting new buildings or drastically converting the inside of existing ones. The West Church of St Nicholas had to be abandoned in 1732 when the roof beams started to crack. Ten years later the roof fell in and thereafter the building was used as a store and stable for Cumberland's troops during the 1745 rebellion. The present West Church, completed in 1755 and designed by James Gibbs, is an extremely well-preserved example of an 18th-century church, with its restrained classical exterior and inside, its box pews, galleries and very prominent pulpit (fig 93). Also in the 18th century, drastic alterations were made to the old Greyfriars church: it was shortened by one bay at the north end to permit easier access through the gateway of Marischal College and an extension was built to the east, creating a T-shaped building, again with box pews and lofts to accommodate members of the College and the town (fig 94).

In the 18th century, too, the whole ecclesiastical structure of Aberdeen became much more complicated, with the beginning of the trend of secession and disruption from the established church, leading to proliferation of church buildings throughout the city. One of the earliest of these was an episcopal church. St Paul's Church, Gallowgate was built in 1720 by a group from the West Church of St Nicholas who wanted to worship according to the liturgy of the Church of England (fig 95). They tried to obtain the lease of the old Trinity Friars' church, still then in existence, but resolved to build a new church when this was not granted. St Paul's was of considerable historic interest as it was visited during its lifetime by John Wesley, Samuel Johnson and Lord Byron. It is also said to have been the first post-Reformation church in Aberdeen to have had an organ, to suit the needs of Anglican worship, and boasted a large three-decker pulpit. It was demolished in the 1860s to make way for a larger, more modern building.

Another 18th-century church still stands at the south end of Exchange Street. Erected in 1794 by a breakaway

95

96

95. *The original St Paul's Episcopal Chapel on the Gallowgate was built in 1721; it was demolished in 1866 to make way for the much larger church which stood here until 1986. It was approached from the Gallowgate through a narrow pend, which opened into the courtyard, from which this 19th-century photograph was taken. The pend was fronted by a magnificent granite archway, erected about 1770.*

96. *The former Trinity Church, erected in 1794, can still be seen behind the modern Guild Street frontage.*

50

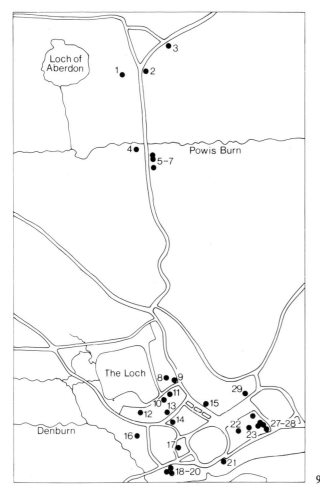

97. *Sites so far excavated in Old and New Aberdeen together with the watching briefs carried out in Old Aberdeen:* 1. *64-72 Don St* 2. *101 High St* 3. *104 High St* 4. *Music Department building* 5-7. *32, 40 & 42 College Bounds* 8. *53-59 Gallowgate* 9. *45-47 Gallowgate* 10. *42 Loch St* 11. *42 St Paul St* 12. *2-16 Harriet St* 13. *42 Upper Kirkgate* 14. *43-57 Upper Kirkgate* 15. *12-26 Broad St/2-28 Queen St* 16. *6 Little Belmont St* 17. *13 Correction Wynd* 18-20. *45-59 Green, 67-71 Green, 12 Martin's Lane* 21. *Shore Brae* 22. *Virginia St, No. 3 Bonded Warehouse* 23. *17 Virginia St* 24. *6-8 Castle Terrace* 25-28. *21-37 Virginia St, Rear of 37 Virginia St, 42 Virginia St, Virginia St Steps/Castle Lane* 29. *Albion Court, 18 Castle St.*

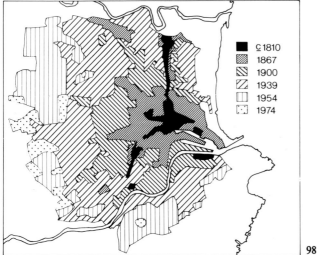

group from the East Church of St Nicholas, it occupied the site of the Trinity Friars' church. Part of the superstructure of Trinity Church, as it was known, can still be seen above a modern warehouse frontage (fig 96).

5. The future of Aberdeen's past

Rescue archaeology has now taken place in Aberdeen for 13 years and in the preceding chapters we have summarized some of our results. Much has been discovered: we now know how properties were laid out, to what purpose they were put, what houses were built there and, to some extent how people lived.

However, a great deal still remains to be discovered. Work has just begun on the last of the major shopping redevelopments to affect the historic core of Aberdeen, along Gallowgate and behind the Upper Kirkgate. Already results have shown the northern expansion of the town to have been related to the growth of industrial activity, probably commencing in the late 13th or early 14th century. Tanning seems to have been carried out extensively as well as metal working. Excavations now beginning behind the Upper Kirkgate should expand our knowledge of domestic settlement and help us to define the western extent of the medieval town and we may even be able to pinpoint the location of the Upper Kirkgate port.

In the coming years as the sites available for redevelopment dwindle, so too will the rate of archaeological exploration. There are, however, a number of areas which still require excavation. The Castlegate, location of the town's main market and the site of many of the main town-houses, has so far yielded little of medieval date but an extensive redevelopment of the southern side of this most important street may yet afford the opportunity to redress this imbalance. A small scale excavation at Shore Brae in 1974 revealed traces of the post-medieval harbour but nothing was found of the medieval waterfront. A major site still exists at Shore Brae so the opportunity may be taken in the near future to re-examine the site and see the extent of Aberdeen's medieval harbour.

Sadly there are other areas of the town where we shall never be able to excavate either because they have been redeveloped prior to this century or because they are in conservation areas. For example, we shall never know in

98. *The growth of the city of Aberdeen. Before 1800 the expansion of New Aberdeen was effectively prohibited by the surrounding natural features. The construction of the viaducts of Union St, George St and King St in the following decade was to enable the growth of settlement to the north and west of the burgh; nevertheless, the new city was slow to expand, and its shape did not begin to change dramatically until the arrival of the railway, and the improvement of road links to the north spurred on the emergence of new industries in the middle of the 19th century. Since then it has grown steadily. This map shows the limits of the main connurbation in about 1970; the present picture is far more complex, with the construction of new estates in the surrounding towns and villages, and the advent of the commuter.*

detail about the castle, or the town's defences, or the structure of the gates or ports guarding access to the town. It is also probably unlikely that we can ever be sure about the town's origins or its area of initial settlement.

Comparison with the results of similar work undertaken in other historic Scottish towns, such as Perth, or on deserted medieval settlements such as Rattray (40 miles north of Aberdeen), may help us to fill in some of these gaps.

When the pressure of excavation has finally ceased, more time can be devoted to doing further research on all the material recovered. This, together with a more thorough examination of the wealth of surviving documentary evidence, will build up a more comprehensive picture of the medieval town in Scotland.

Finally, although our efforts to date have concentrated on excavation within the historic burghs of Old and New Aberdeen we must not lose sight of the fact that the towns are only one aspect of medieval life in the region. They did not exist in a vacuum and it is imperative that we should examine and attempt to understand their relationship with the rural hinterland. In future years, then, we shall also initiate projects to examine the nature and complexities of medieval rural settlement around Aberdeen and see how it contributed to the town's growth and development.

Acknowledgements

Aberdeen Art Gallery and Museums Department is grateful to the Scottish Development Department (Historic Buildings and Monuments) for financing the excavations which are presented in this book.

Many organisations and individuals have contributed towards the preparation and publication of this volume, notably the specialists and consultants who have given advice during excavation and post-excavation work on sites in the City District. Many developers, large and small, have given us access to sites and have often provided us with services. A particular debt is owed to members of the City of Aberdeen Department of Planning and Building Control for their co-operation in monitoring threatened sites in the city. The analysis of the human skeletal remains from the Carmelite Friary was carried out at the Department of Anatomy, Marischal College, Aberdeen, and the section on health is based on a text by Juliet Cross of that Department.

For permission to reproduce photographs the authors are indebted to Aberdeen City Libraries (fig 28, 35, 36, 79, 83, 86, 89, 92, 95); the Bibliothèque Nationale, Paris (fig 31); the British Library (figs 52, 53); the Royal Commission on the Ancient and Historical Monuments of Scotland (Crown Copyright: fig 27). Fig 43 is reproduced from Cartularium Ecclesiae S. Nicholai Aberdonensis, Vol I, New Spalding Club, Aberdeen 1888. Figs 7b, 8, 10, 46, 47, 62, 64, 64a, 66 are photographs taken by Roger Brown, figs 68-72 by Juliet Cross, figs 11, 14 by Dave Evans and fig 9 by Donald Thompson.

99

99. *17th, 18th and 19th-century houses in the High Street in Old Aberdeen, displaying a broad range of architectural features and styles resulting from centuries of growth and development. Some houses are built parallel to the street, whilst others (like the one on the left) are set at right-angles to it. They range in height from single-storeyed cottages, such as Grant's Place (just visible in the centre of the left-hand side of the street – next to the minibus), to the three-storeyed buildings on the right, with their gabled dormer windows. The chimneys vary from elegant chamfered stacks on the left, to the large multi-flued Georgian stacks on the right.*